I0825012

CANTINA Mexicana

CANTINA Mexicana

Over 70 recipes for tacos, tostadas, burritos, margaritas and more!

rps

RYLAND PETERS & SMALL

Senior Designer Toni Kay
Senior Editor Abi Waters
Head of Production Patricia Harrington
Creative Director Leslie Harrington
Editorial Director Julia Charles

Indexer Vanessa Bird

First published in 2026 by
Ryland Peters & Small,
20–21 Jockey's Fields,
London WC1R 4BW
and
1452 Davis Bugg Road,
Warrenton, NC 27589

www.rylandpeters.com
email: euregulations@rylandpeters.com

Note: Some recipes in this book have been previously published by Ryland Peters & Small. See page 144 for full text and photography credits.

ISBN: 978-1-78879-754-2

10 9 8 7 6 5 4 3 2 1

A CIP record for this book is available from the British Library.

US Library of Congress cataloging-in-publication data has been applied for.
The authorised representative in the EEA is Authorised Rep Compliance Ltd., Ground Floor, 71 Lower Baggot Street, Dublin, D02 P593, Ireland
www.arccompliance.com

Printed and bound in China.

NOTES

- Both British (Metric) and American (Imperial plus US cup) measurements are included in these recipes for your convenience – however it is important to work with one set of measurements and not alternate between the two within a recipe.
- All spoon measurements are level unless specified.
- All eggs are medium (UK) or large (US), unless specified as large, in which case US extra-large should be used. Uncooked or partially cooked eggs should not be served to the elderly or frail, young children, pregnant women or those with compromised immune systems.
- Ovens should be preheated to the specified temperatures. We recommend using an oven thermometer. If using a fan-assisted oven, adjust temperatures according to the manufacturer's instructions.
- When a recipe calls for the grated zest of citrus fruit, buy unwaxed fruit and wash well before using. If you can only find treated fruit, scrub well in warm soapy water before using.

Contents

MEXICAN INGREDIENTS
Tomatoes, limes, chillies/chiles and spices form the basis of Mexican cooking, not forgetting the varieties of rice and beans that round out dishes and give them an unmistakable sustenance.

Introduction

Get ready to spice up your kitchen and bring the vibrant flavours of Mexico to your table with this tantalizing collection of recipes. Whether you're here for the temptingly tasty tacos, the fiery fajitas or the irresistible margaritas, you've come to the right place. No restaurant equipment needed, no culinary degree required – just a love of good food, a bit of curiosity and maybe a lime or two.

At the heart of Mexican cooking is balance – the bright zing of lime against the smoky depth of chipotle, the sweetness of corn paired with the earthiness of beans and the complex layers of chillies/chiles, herbs and spices that blend perfectly together. The cool creaminess of guacamole contrasts perfectly with the fiery bite of salsa to create a real celebration of colour and flavour.

The recipes in this book feature the familiar Mexican staples of tacos and tostados, burritos and quesadillas, salsas and sides, and not forgetting the all-important margarita. Sample the very best fish tacos, birria beef burritos and chicken quesadillas, before you dive head first into the Margarita and More chapter to pair each dish with the perfect drink. Impressive bakes and desserts are also included to round off your Mexican feast to perfection.

Everything is taken a step further with some unmissable Mexican fusion dishes, such as BLT Tacos, Philly Steak Chimichangas and Caramelized Apple Burritos to provide a well-rounded balance of dishes that will fuel your love of Mexican cooking.

So grab your apron, crank up the mariachi and get ready to chop, stir and taste your way through dishes that are as colourful as a Mexican mercado. Cook, laugh and maybe even dance a little as you celebrate and discover the best of Mexican cuisine.

Greetings from
TIJUANA
IN OLD MEXICO
Old Mexico

Chips, Dips & Snacks

Homemade Tortilla Chips

Preparing your own tortilla chips may seem like a bit of a hassle, but this homemade version puts the store-bought variety to shame. Once you've got the hang of the timing, it is really very simple.

vegetable oil, for frying
8 corn tortillas, cut into eighths
½ teaspoon sea salt

MAKES LOTS!

Pour some vegetable oil into a deep saucepan until it comes 2 cm/¾ inches up the side of the pan. Set over medium heat and leave until the oil is very hot but not smoking.

Carefully drop in the tortilla triangles, in batches of 10, and fry for 30 seconds, turning the chips gently and often with tongs to prevent them burning.

Use tongs or a slotted spoon to remove the chips from the pan and allow to drain on paper towels. Repeat the process until all the chips have been fried.

Toss with the salt and serve warm.

Spiced Pumpkin Seeds

These irresistible salty snacks provide a great and authentic alternative to the normal nuts and olives. They also make a good ingredient in sauces and dressings, so it's worth getting the hang of making them.

90 g/¾ cup shelled pumpkin seeds
¼ teaspoon paprika
pinch of sea salt
1 teaspoon vegetable oil
1 lime, halved (optional)

MAKES A BOWLFUL

Put the pumpkin seeds in a dry frying pan/skillet over low heat. Stir continuously for 10 minutes, taking care not to let them burn.

Remove from the heat, add the paprika, salt and oil and mix well. Immediately transfer to a bowl to prevent further cooking.

Serve plain or with a squeeze of lime juice. They work well as a snack or as an accompaniment to your meal.

CORONA

Layered 'Nacho' Dip with tortilla chips

One of the all-time favourite sharing plates is nachos – tortilla chips are served piled high with tomato salsa, guacamole, sour cream and grated cheese, then warmed under a grill/broiler. This dip version is layered up in a bowl and then warmed, ready to scoop out with crunchy tortilla chips. Perfect for a Mexican fiesta celebration!

GUACAMOLE

6 ripe avocados, halved and pitted
½ red onion
handful of freshly chopped coriander/cilantro
2 fresh red chillies/chiles, deseeded and finely chopped
freshly squeezed juice of 2 limes
2–3 pinches of sea salt flakes
Tabasco and cayenne pepper (optional), to taste

TOMATO SALSA

6 ripe medium tomatoes
freshly squeezed juice of 1 lime
10g/⅛ oz. fresh coriander/cilantro
2 spring onions/scallions, trimmed
1 fresh red chilli/chile, trimmed and deseeded
sea salt and freshly ground black pepper

TO ASSEMBLE

200 ml/7 fl. oz. sour cream
125 g/4½ oz. strong cheese, such as mature/sharp Cheddar, grated
handful of jarred jalapeño slices (optional)
Homemade Tortilla Chips (see page 10), to serve

SERVES 6

Scoop the flesh out of the avocados with a tablespoon into a shallow bowl. Add the onion, coriander and chillies. Add the lime juice, then mash everything together with a fork, leaving the texture quite chunky. Season with salt to taste. Add a few dashes of Tabasco and a few pinches of cayenne, if using. Cover with cling film/plastic wrap until ready to use.

For the salsa, cut the tomatoes in half then scoop out and discard the seeds. Put in a blender or food processor along with the lime juice, coriander, spring onions and chilli and pulse for a few seconds to roughly chop the tomatoes. Season to taste with salt and pepper. Cover with cling film until ready to use.

To assemble the dip, spoon the guacamole into a shallow serving bowl and spread out in a thick layer. Top with the tomato salsa, then spoon over the sour cream, scatter over the grated cheese and finish with jalapeños, if using.

Gently warm under a preheated grill/broiler just until the cheese starts to melt. Serve straight away with the tortilla chips.

Loaded Black Bean & Sweetcorn Nachos

Nachos marry particularly well with a margarita cocktail or a gin and tonic and are much more exciting than simply crunching through a packet of crisps on a Saturday night. This recipe should be enough for four people, but in fairness, that would probably be four very restrained, polite people – so you might want to double up on the quantities.

- 1 x 200 g/7 oz. bag tortilla chips
- 200 g/7 oz. cherry tomatoes, coarsely chopped
- 300-g/10½-oz. can sweetcorn/corn kernels, drained
- 1 x 400-g/14-oz. can black beans, drained and rinsed
- 1 x small jar jalapeño peppers, drained and sliced
- bunch of spring onions/scallions, thinly sliced
- 200 g/2¼ cups extra mature/sharp Cheddar cheese, grated/shredded
- sour cream, to serve

SERVES 4

Preheat the oven to 190°C (375°F) Gas 5.

Scatter a handful of tortilla chips over the base of a large sheet pan. Scatter over a handful of chopped cherry tomatoes, then some sweetcorn and finally some black beans.

Dot with jalapeño slices, scatter over some spring onions and then sprinkle the cheese generously over the top. Repeat these layers until you have used everything up.

Transfer to the oven and bake for 4–5 minutes until the cheese is melted and gooey.

Serve with sour cream.

Chorizo & Three-bean Smoky Nacho Platter

3 wholemeal/whole-wheat tortillas, cut into triangles (or 100 g/3½ cups blue corn tortilla chips)
oil, for spraying and frying
190 g/1½ cups chorizo, roughly chopped
1 red onion, roughly chopped
1 tablespoon ground cumin
1 large bunch of coriander/cilantro, stems finely chopped, leaves reserved
1 red chilli/chile, finely chopped
2 tablespoons tomato paste
1 tablespoon smoked chipotle paste
2 garlic cloves, crushed
1 teaspoon dried oregano
½ teaspoon smoked paprika
100 ml/scant ½ cup vegetable stock
400-g/14-oz. can black beans
400-g/14-oz. can kidney beans
400-g/14-oz. can aduki beans
400-g/14-oz. can chopped tomatoes
1 tablespoon Worcestershire sauce

TO SERVE
50 g/½ cup sliced olives
handful of grated mozzarella
100 g/½ cup queso fresca or crumbled feta cheese
Greek yogurt
jalapeños
Guacamole (see page 13)
two baking sheets lightly sprayed with oil

SERVES 6

This is a twist on a Mexican classic and can be a great vegetarian option if you omit the chorizo and add an extra teaspoon of smoked paprika. The smoky bean mix can also become the perfect topping to a bowl of rice the next day.

If using tortillas, preheat the oven to 200°C (400°F) Gas 6. Arrange the tortilla triangles in a single layer on the baking sheets. Lightly spray with oil and bake for 5–6 minutes or until golden. Cool on a wire rack.

Heat the oil in a large frying pan/skillet over medium heat. Add the chorizo and onion and cook, stirring, for 5 minutes or until the onion is soft. Increase the heat to high. Add the ground cumin, coriander stems and chilli and cook, stirring, for 1 minute. Add the tomato paste, chipotle paste, garlic, oregano and smoked paprika and stir for a further minute. Stir in the vegetable stock, beans, canned tomatoes and Worcestershire sauce, bring to the boil and gently boil for 10 minutes or until thickened. (Beans can be made the day before and kept in the fridge, reheat before using.)

To assemble, preheat the grill/broiler to medium/high and arrange the nachos on a large plate, top with the beans, olives and a handful of grated mozzarella. Place under the grill/broiler until the mozzarella has melted. Serve with the reserved coriander leaves and crumbled queso fresca, and with yogurt, jalapeños and Guacamole on the side.

Note: This recipe deliberately makes a large quantity of the smoky beans as they are so good eaten as leftovers!

Green & Red Memelitas

You will find memelitas among all the late-night street vendors throughout cities in Mexico. Perfect as a snack, canapé or light lunch.

125 ml/½ cup vegetable oil
½ onion, finely chopped

CORN TORTILLA DOUGH
300 g/2 cups masa harina
300 ml/1¼ cups warm water
¼ teaspoon sea salt

TOPPINGS
any of your favourite salsas or Refried Beans (see page 98)
200 g/2 cups crumbled feta cheese
clean plastic bag
tortilla press (optional)

MAKES 8

Heat the oil in a small, deep saucepan. Once hot, remove from the heat and add the chopped onion. Set aside until later.

Make the dough: put the masa harina, water and salt in a mixing bowl and mix well for 5 minutes. Divide into 8 equal pieces and roll into balls. Place one ball of dough in the middle of the plastic bag and fold the bag in half over the dough.

Flatten the dough using a tortilla press or, if you don't have a tortilla press, pat a large saucepan down on top of the plastic-covered dough repeatedly, pressing down firmly and evenly. Now put aside the pan and pat firmly a few times with the palm of your hand to flatten the dough even further.

Very carefully peel back the plastic from the top of the dough, making sure the dough does not tear, then loosely replace it. Finally, flip it over and gently peel back the plastic. The disc should be about ½ cm/¾ inch thick.

Heat a non-stick frying pan/skillet over medium heat, then cook each disc of dough for 1 minute. Flip over and cook for another minute until cooked through, then set aside and allow to cool slightly while you cook the remaining discs.

Take a disc and, using your index finger and thumb, pinch the edge of the tortilla all the way round and make a few pinches in the middle. Repeat with the remaining tortillas.

Return the frying pan to medium heat. Place a tortilla in the pan, pour 1 teaspoon of the reserved onion oil on top and spread it evenly. Heat for about 1 minute, then spread over a little of your favourite salsa or refried beans. Sprinkle some cheese on top. Remove from the pan and repeat with all the remaining memelitas. If your pan is big enough you can heat more than one at a time.

Let your guests choose their favourite memelitas.

Beer-battered Avocado Dippers

When it comes to using avocados in Mexican cooking, deep-frying is not what immediately springs to mind. However, this is one of those healthy/naughty treats! Take something super-healthy and then deep-fry it in a beer batter ... what's not to love? The combination of the crispy batter and the soft avocado centre is amazing, even before you dip it into the creamy chipotle mayo.

6–8 ripe avocados
vegetable oil, for deep-frying

CHIPOTLE MAYONNAISE
150 g/¾ cup mayonnaise
2 teaspoons chipotle paste
1 garlic clove, peeled

BATTER
165 g/1⅓ cups self-raising flour/self-rising flour
1 teaspoon sea salt
1 teaspoon cumin
1 teaspoon dried oregano
1½ teaspoons paprika
½ teaspoon freshly ground black pepper
1 teaspoon ground avocado leaf powder
1 teaspoon baking powder
1 bottle (330 ml/11 fl oz) Sol beer, or substitute your lager of choice

SERVES 6–8

First, make the chipotle mayonnaise. Put all the ingredients in a blender and blend for about 1 minute until smooth. Set aside until ready to serve.

To make the batter, mix together all the dry ingredients until they are well combined. Gently stir in the beer until you have a smooth batter and then put to one side.

Cut the avocados in half, peel them and remove the stones. Slice each half into 3–4 pieces lengthways, depending on their size.

Pour enough oil into a medium saucepan to reach halfway up the side and heat until hot but not smoking.

Working with one avocado at a time, dip the slices in the batter until well covered, then carefully lower into the oil – it's best to use a slotted spoon to do this to avoid spitting oil.

Fry each batch for about 1 minute so that the batter is golden coloured, but no darker, and crispy. Remove with a slotted spoon and place on a plate lined with paper towels to soak up any excess oil. Repeat with the remaining avocado slices.

Transfer the chipotle mayonnaise to a serving bowl and place on a large serving plate. Arrange the avocado slices on the plate, serve and watch your friends' amazement when they try this dish!

Chorizo Breakfast Nacho Skillet

What can be said about breakfast nachos? They are perfect for any time of day. Using spicy chorizo sausage, scrambled egg and a blend of three cheeses, this recipe easily transitions from breakfast to dinner. The textures are fantastic and the dish has plenty of spicy Mexican flair.

450 g/1 lb. chorizo sausage
½ white onion, chopped
5 eggs, beaten
4 ripe tomatoes, chopped
Homemade Tortilla Chips (see page 10)
2 jarred jalapeño peppers, sliced
225 g/8 oz. pre-packaged 'Mexican blend' grated/shredded cheese or a mixture of freshly grated/shredded mature/sharp Cheddar, mild Cheddar/Colby and Gouda/Monterey Jack
125 ml/½ cup sour cream

SERVES 4

Preheat the oven to 180°C (350°F) Gas 4.

Cook the chorizo in a frying pan/skillet over medium heat for about 5 minutes until crumbled and evenly browned. Drain and set aside.

Cook the onion in the same frying pan/skillet until soft, then stir in the eggs and scramble with the onion. Mix in the tomatoes and continue to cook and stir until the eggs are nearly set. Remove from the heat.

Spread a layer of tortilla chips into a medium cast-iron frying pan/skillet. Scatter the chorizo and the scrambled egg mixture over the chips. Top with jalapeño slices and cover with the grated cheese.

Bake in the preheated oven for 7–10 minutes, until the cheese is melted. Serve hot and eat with your fingers!

Jalapeño Poppers

Jalapeños are ideal for this recipe. They have a juicy flesh that tastes delicious when combined with cheese. If they are not available, I would suggest using red Cherry Bomb chillies/chiles, which are a little sweeter and often a little hotter too! These poppers will whet your appetite at the start of a barbecue.

20 jalapeño peppers
140 g/1¼ cups grated/shredded mature/sharp Cheddar cheese
50 g/⅓ cup plain/all-purpose flour
1 egg, beaten
sunflower oil, for deep frying
cooking thermometer (optional)

MAKES 20

Slit the jalapeños along one side and carefully remove the seeds. Stuff them generously with the grated cheddar.

Put the flour in one shallow bowl and the beaten egg in another. Roll the Jalapeños in the flour, dip in the egg and then coat once more with flour, ensuring that they are completely covered.

Half-fill a large saucepan with oil. Heat until the oil reaches 190°C (375°F) on a cooking thermometer. If you don't have a cooking thermometer, the oil is ready when a 2.5-cm/1-inch cube of white bread dropped into it browns in less than 60 seconds.

Fry the jalapeños in small batches for 6–7 minutes until golden. Remove with a slotted spoon and drain on paper towels.

Chicken Taquitos

Taquito (also known as a *flauta*) in Spanish means 'little taco'. They are tacos filled with various ingredients, rolled like a cigar, then fried until crisp. These chicken taquitos can be made using corn or flour tortillas, although corn is more traditional. Cheese is another good addition to the filling and, for a vegetarian option, herby mashed potato is a popular alternative.

2 boneless, skinless chicken breasts
2 garlic cloves, crushed
¼ onion, chopped
¼ teaspoon sea salt
12 corn tortillas
vegetable oil, for frying

SERVE WITH
½ romaine lettuce, shredded
Pico de Gallo (see page 93)
125 ml/½ cup sour cream
200 g/7 oz queso fresco or feta cheese
36 cocktail sticks/toothpicks

SERVES 3–4

Pour 1 litre/4 cups water into a saucepan and bring to the boil. Add the chicken, garlic, onion and salt and simmer for 7–8 minutes or until the chicken is completely cooked.

Lift out the chicken and set aside to cool. Reserve the onion and garlic, and discard the cooking liquid. Shred the cooled chicken and mix with the cooked onion and garlic.

Take one tortilla and heat in a dry, non-stick frying pan/ skillet until softened and flexible.

Spoon a little shredded chicken onto the warmed tortilla, just slightly to the side of centre. Roll the tortilla into a cylinder and secure it with 3 cocktail sticks, gently pushing them through the cylinder. Repeat with all the remaining tortillas and chicken.

Pour vegetable oil into a deep frying pan to a depth of about 2 cm/¾ inches. Heat over medium heat until the oil is hot but not smoking.

Carefully drop in the taquitos in batches of 3–4 and fry for 12 minutes until golden, turning gently and occasionally to prevent them from burning.

Using tongs or a slotted spoon, remove the taquitos from the pan and allow to drain on paper towels. When the taquitos are cool enough to handle, remove the cocktail sticks.

Put a little shredded lettuce on each plate, add 3–4 taquitos, top with Pico de Gallo, sour cream and crumbled cheese.

Chilquiles

This is a very traditional Mexican dish but one which has its variations and twists in every region of Mexico. These fried corn tortillas are usually served for breakfast or lunch and are a great way to make use of any leftover tortillas and salsas.

- vegetable oil, for frying
- 10 corn tortillas, cut into eighths
- 2 tomatoes
- 5 dried Chiles de Arbol (or other hot dried red chillies), seeded and stalks removed
- 1 teaspoon paprika
- ½ onion, finely chopped
- 2 medium eggs
- pinch of sea salt
- 100 g/1 cup grated/shredded Cheddar cheese

SERVES 4

Pour some vegetable oil into a deep saucepan until it comes 2 cm/¾ inches up the side of the pan. Set over medium heat and leave until the oil is very hot but not smoking.

Carefully drop in the tortilla triangles, in batches of 10, and fry for about 30 seconds, turning the chips gently and often with tongs to prevent them from burning.

Using the tongs or a slotted spoon, remove the chips from the pan and allow to drain on paper towels. Repeat the process until all the chips have been fried. Reserve the oil.

Place 500 ml/2 cups water, the tomatoes and chillies in a saucepan and boil for 5 minutes. Allow to cool for 10 minutes, then transfer all of it to a food processor with the paprika and whizz for 2 minutes or until smooth. Set aside.

Take 1 tablespoon of the reserved cooking oil and put in a large saucepan over medium heat. Add the tortilla chips and onions to the pan, then add the eggs. Using a large spoon, very gently stir the mixture for 1 minute until the egg is cooked, but be careful not to break the fried tortilla chips.

Add the blended sauce, as well as the salt and cook for about 3–5 minutes or until the sauce is heated through – avoid overcooking or the tortillas will turn soggy. They need to mix well with the sauce but still retain a little of their crunchiness.

Preheat the grill/broiler to medium.

Transfer the chilaquiles to an ovenproof dish and sprinkle the cheese over the top. Grill/broil for 1–2 minutes until the cheese has melted.

Note: Serve with Refried Beans (see page 98), if you like.

FLOR SILVESTRE

Tacos & Tostados

Beef Brisket Barbacoa Tacos

Barbacoa is one of the most traditional and evocative Mexican meals as it is usually served at a celebration. Often a whole sheep or goat would be used, but here this version uses beef brisket.

100 g/3½ oz. red onions
300 g/10½ oz. large tomatoes
2 kg/4½ lb trimmed beef brisket
4 tablespoons paprika
2 teaspoons ground cumin
1 tablespoon chopped chipotle chilli/chile
2 teaspoons avocado leaf powder
3 teaspoons sea salt
1 teaspoon freshly ground black pepper
2 teaspoons rice vinegar

SERVE WITH

2 limes, cut into wedges
12 flour or corn tortillas, warmed
1 avocado, peeled, stoned and diced
Salsa Roja (see page 90)

SERVES 4

Slice the red onions about 1 cm/½ inch thick. Slice the tomatoes into wedges.

Cut the beef into big chunks and place in a large lidded saucepan. Pour 2 litres/8 cups water into the pan and add the onions, tomatoes, paprika, cumin, chipotle chilli, avocado leaf powder, salt, pepper and rice vinegar. Mix together with a large spoon.

Place the pan over high heat and bring to the boil, then cover with a lid and reduce the heat to low. Simmer gently for 3 hours, stirring occasionally and making sure the pan does not boil dry.

Shred the meat inside the saucepan using tongs or a fork. Just before serving, squeeze one of the limes over the shredded meat.

Put the meat on a tortilla, add avocado, some salsa and a squeeze of lime juice.

Note: The avocado tree is known almost everywhere in the world because of its fruit, but the leaves are a wonderful, aromatic addition to many dishes too. The dried leaves give off a smell similar to anise and go well with beans and some stewed meats.

JARRITOS
MEXICAN
20
2
EL DIABLITO

Roasted Pork Belly Tacos

In Mexico, *carnitas* means 'little meats' and refers to the fact that you first slow-cook the meat, and then chop it into small pieces before crisping it up in a pan at the last minute. This method results in beautiful and tender meat that has a little bite to it. Add in the juice and zest of the orange and you have a really special, citrus-sweet flavour.

1 kg/2¼ lb. pork belly
2½ teaspoons sea salt
2 tablespoons vegetable oil
zest and juice of 2 oranges

SERVE WITH
12 flour or corn tortillas, warmed
Pico de Gallo (see page 93)
Chipotle Slaw (see page 101)
2–3 spring onions/scallions, thinly sliced
50 g/2 oz. radishes, thinly sliced
your favourite salsa

SERVES 3–4

Preheat the oven to 220°C (425°F) Gas 7.

Pour 500 ml/2 cups of water into a deep roasting tray. Place a rack in the roasting tray, then place the pork on the rack to prevent it touching the bottom of the tray. Cover the pork evenly with 2 teaspoons of the salt. Cover the whole container with a lid or foil and bake in the preheated oven for 1½ hours.

When the pork is cooked through, transfer to a chopping board. Discard any bones or cartilage and chop the meat into strips about 5 mm/¼ inch thick and 5 cm/2 inches long.

Heat the oil in a saucepan, add the meat and sauté for about 5 minutes to crisp up. Add the remaining salt and the orange zest and juice and continue cooking, stirring continuously, for another 5–7 minutes.

Place some pork in the centre of each warmed tortilla and top with Pico de Gallo, Chipotle Slaw, spring onions, radishes and salsa.

Pinto Bean & Chorizo Tacos

Pinto beans are a staple of Mexican cooking and a great source of high-quality fibre and protein. You will be hard pushed to find any restaurant in Mexico that will not serve its own version of this classic. This recipe uses paprika to add flavour and colour, and then the whole dish is pepped up with the addition of some sliced chorizo.

- **175 g/1 cup dried pinto beans**
- **1 tablespoon vegetable oil**
- **150 g/5 oz. chorizo, chopped or sliced**
- **¼ onion, finely chopped**
- **1 small garlic clove, finely chopped**
- **2 teaspoons paprika**
- **½ teaspoon sea salt**

SERVE WITH

- **8–12 corn or flour tortillas, warmed**
- **200 g/7 oz. queso fresco or feta cheese, crumbled (optional)**
- **freshly chopped coriander/cilantro (optional)**
- **150 g/5 oz. chorizo, sliced**
- **Chilli Tomato Salsa (see page 97)**

SERVES 4

Soak the pinto beans overnight in plenty of cold water to soften them. After soaking, drain them and put into a deep saucepan with 1.5 litres/6 cups of fresh water.

Bring to the boil and boil rapidly for 10 minutes, then turn the heat down to low and cook for 2–2½ hours. Put a lid on the saucepan but do not cover fully – just tilt the lid so that there is a gap to allow steam to escape. Keep an eye on it just in case you need to add a little more water. At the end, you should be able to crush the beans easily between your fingers – but please don't try this when they are hot! If they still have some bite, cook for a little longer, adding more water if necessary.

Heat the oil in a medium saucepan, add the chorizo pieces, onion and garlic and sweat for about 1 minute.

Add the cooked beans and the paprika and cook for 10 minutes over medium-low heat, using a potato masher to mash the beans continuously. The beans and chorizo should not be runny. Add the salt to taste.

Fill the warmed tortillas with the refried bean and chorizo mixture and stack next to each other on a serving plate. Now sprinkle the cheese and coriander, if using, onto each taco and serve with the additional chorizo and salsa alongside.

BLT Tacos

A slight departure from the traditional Mexican taco here, but the combination of crispy bacon with the fresh cucumber salsa is what makes this truly spectacular. Think light lunch on a hot, summer's day, or refreshing appetizer before a barbecue feast.

2 teaspoons vegetable oil
8 rashers/slices of bacon

TO SERVE
1 Romaine lettuce
2 tomatoes, chopped
sliced cucumber
finely sliced red onion
your favourite tomato salsa
1 tablespoon freshly chopped parsley

SERVES 3-4

Place the vegetable oil in a frying pan/skillet over medium-high heat and fry the bacon for 6–7 minutes. Turn the bacon over several times.

Put the bacon on a plate lined with paper towels to absorb any excess oil.

Wash the lettuce leaves and remove the stems.

Take a leaf of lettuce and place it in a bowl shape on a plate. Put a rasher or two of bacon in the middle of the leaf, top with some tomato, cucumber and red onion and spoon over some salsa. Scatter over the parsley.

Spinach, Chorizo & Potato Tacos

Children will love these potato tacos. The chorizo adds a touch of spice and great colour to the potatoes and spinach, making it an all-round winner whatever your age!

100 g/3½ oz. chorizo
1 medium potato
1 red onion
2 tablespoons vegetable oil
100 g/2 cups baby spinach leaves
pinch of sea salt
pinch of white pepper

SERVE WITH
bunch of watercress
100 g/3½ oz. radishes, thinly sliced
5–6 corn or flour tortillas, warmed
200 g/1½ cups crumbled queso fresco or feta cheese
Salsa Rojo (see page 90)

SERVES 2–3

Cut the chorizo into slices about 5 mm/¼ inch thick.

Peel the potato and cut it into small strips. Thinly slice the red onion.

Heat the oil in a saucepan over medium heat, add the chorizo slices and cook for 2 minutes. Add the potato and fry for 6–8 minutes until cooked. Add the onion, spinach, salt and white pepper and cook for another 1–2 minutes, then put them to one side.

Place the watercress and radish slices in two separate bowls on the table. Place the chorizo mixture in the middle of the warmed tortillas and add the crumbled cheese. Add a dollop of salsa and serve.

Modelo

Chipotle Chicken Tacos

Although tacos are at the heart of Mexican cooking, chicken is not as common a filling as pork or beef. Using chicken breast in a smoky chipotle marinade will add a different flavour dimension to your usual Mexican feast.

400 g/14 oz. chicken breast fillets
8 x 15-cm/6-inch corn or flour tortillas

CHIPOTLE MARINADE
1 tablespoon Chipotle chilli paste
1 teaspoon ground cinnamon
1 teaspoon ground cumin
3 garlic cloves
1 tablespoon dried oregano
1 tablespoon paprika
½ teaspoon sea salt
125 ml/½ cup vegetable oil

TO SERVE
handful of shredded Romaine lettuce
Pico de Gallo (page 93)
sour cream

SERVES 4

Put all the ingredients for the chipotle marinade, along with 125 ml/½ cup water, in a food processor and whizz until smooth. Put the chicken breast in a bowl, add the marinade and mix well. Cover, refrigerate and marinate for 2–4 hours.

When you are ready to start cooking, preheat the grill/broiler to high.

Grill/broil the chicken for about 10 minutes, turning halfway through, until cooked through. Cut the cooked chicken into strips.

Place a dry frying pan/skillet over high heat. Warm each tortilla for about 20–30 seconds on each side.

Layer up the ingredients over the tortillas: lettuce, Pico de Gallo, sour cream and the chicken.

Eggs & Ham Tacos

Most Mexican households start their day with a breakfast of eggs. As with many such recipes, it is the combination of creamy eggs with a zesty salsa that provides the perfect balance for the morning. Having salsa with breakfast doesn't mean it has to be spicy – just use your favourite salsa. Check out the Huevos Rancheros (see page 59) for another popular Mexican breakfast dish.

6 eggs
1 tablespoon of your favourite salsa, plus extra to serve
2 tablespoons vegetable oil
125 g/4½ oz. (6–8 thin slices) ham, chopped into pieces
1 teaspoon sea salt

SERVE WITH

8–12 flour or corn tortillas, warmed
100 g/1 cup grated/shredded cheese (ideally Monterey Jack or mild Cheddar)

SERVES 3–4

Break the eggs into a bowl, add the salsa and whisk for about 30 seconds.

Heat the oil in a saucepan over low-medium heat, then add the chopped ham and salt and sauté for a few seconds. Add the beaten eggs and cook for about 1–2 minutes, stirring gently.

While the eggs are cooking, heat the tortillas. Place the warmed tortillas on the table together with the eggs, a bowl of salsa and the grated cheese, and let everyone help themselves.

Prawn Tacos with butter, garlic & paprika

Generally fresh fish is delivered daily to the markets in Mexico and seafood restaurants are everywhere. Hence, prawn/shrimp tacos are a popular dish, especially enjoyed in the sunshine with an ice-cold beer.

15 g/1 tablespoon butter
2 garlic cloves, chopped
200 g/6½ oz. shelled raw or cooked prawns/shrimp
pinch of paprika
4 x 15-cm/6-inch corn or flour tortillas

TO SERVE

150 g/2 cups shredded Romaine lettuce
Pico de Gallo (see page 93)
Chipotle Mayonnaise (see page 52)
1 lemon, cut into wedges

SERVES 2

Melt the butter in a frying pan/skillet over low heat and fry the garlic, prawns and paprika for about 2–4 minutes, stirring occasionally, until the prawns are cooked through.

Place a dry frying pan over high heat. Warm each tortilla for about 20–30 seconds on each side.

Layer up the ingredients over the tortillas: lettuce, Pico de Gallo, prawns and chipotle mayonnaise. Serve with lemon wedges to squeeze over.

Fish Tacos with chipotle-lime crema

This is a baked version of a Baja fish taco. What you miss in fatty crunch from the lack of batter is made up for by the winning addition of guacamole and chipotle-lime crema. It's the perfect taste of summer.

700 g/1 lb. 9 oz. skinless white fish fillets

2 handfuls coriander/cilantro leaves and stems, chopped

1 handful pumpkin seeds/ pepitas

2 tablespoons olive oil

zest of ½ lime

CHIPOTLE-LIME CREMA

1 dried chipotle chilli plus 2 tablespoons just-boiled water (or substitute chipotle powder, or smoked barbecue sauce with cayenne pepper)

4 tablespoons crème fraîche, sour cream or natural yogurt

juice and zest of ½ lime

a few coriander/cilantro leaves

TO SERVE

warmed corn or wheat soft tortillas or tacos (2–3 per person)

Guacamole (see page 90)

4 large handfuls shredded white cabbage

jalapeños, to taste

sea salt

SERVES 4

First, make the chipotle-lime crema. Split the dried chipotle chilli and shake out most of the seeds. Dry-toast it in a frying pan/skillet until it smells nutty. Cover it with just-boiled water and steep for 15 minutes. Purée the chilli and the steeping water until smooth.

Put 2 teaspoons of the chipotle purée in the bottom of a blender. Add the crème fraîche and lime zest and juice. Process until smooth and top with a few coriander/cilantro leaves.

Preheat the oven to 200°C (400°F) Gas 6.

Dry the fish fillets well and place them on a baking sheet. Cover them with coriander leaves, pumpkin seeds, a drizzle of olive oil and the zest of half a lime (use the juice in the guacamole).

Bake the fish for 10–12 minutes, until the flesh is opaque, or wrap in foil and grill on the barbecue. Break each cooked fillet into thirds (keeping the pumpkin seeds and coriander with each one). Place the fish on a serving platter with the tortillas, guacamole, shredded cabbage, chipotle-lime crema and jalapeños, and assemble your own tacos.

Note: Any remaining chipotle purée can be frozen in an ice cube tray, so there's some on hand next time you make tacos, burritos, enchiladas or pulled pork.

LA SIRENA

Salmon & Spicy Black Bean Tacos

A deliciously different fish taco that combines succulent oven-baked salmon with satisfying mashed black beans, all pepped up with ginger and garlic.

BEANS

165 g/1 cup dried black beans
3 tablespoons vegetable oil
1–2 dried chillies/chiles de árbol, cut into small pieces
1/4 onion, finely chopped
1 garlic clove, chopped
1/2 teaspoon sea salt
1 tablespoon ground avocado leaf powder

SALMON

splash of olive oil
500 g/1 lb 2 oz. fresh salmon fillets, skin removed
1/2 teaspoon finely grated fresh ginger
pinch of white pepper
2–3 garlic cloves, finely chopped

SERVE WITH

12 flour or corn tortillas, warmed
pickled red onions (store-bought)
fresh jalapeños, seeds and stems removed, thinly sliced

SERVES 4

Put the dried beans in a deep saucepan with 2 litres/8 cups water and bring to the boil. Turn the heat down to low, partially cover and simmer gently for 2 hours. Check every 30 minutes to be sure there is still enough water and stir so that the beans don't stick to the bottom of the pan.

After 2 hours, heat the oil in a large saucepan over a medium heat. Add the dried chilli, onion, garlic, salt and ground avocado leaf powder and fry gently for 15–20 seconds. Mix together with the cooked black beans. Transfer the beans and cooking water to a blender and blend for 1 minute. Tip into a saucepan and bring them back to simmer over medium heat for 2–3 minutes – this will bring out the rich and aromatic flavour. Put to one side to cool.

Preheat the oven to 220°C (425°F) Gas 7.

Line an ovenproof dish with foil and add a splash of olive oil. Place the salmon on the foil. Add the grated ginger and white pepper and scatter over the garlic, gently pushing it into the fillets. Bake in the preheated oven for 20–25 minutes.

Once cooked, gently break the salmon into bite-sized pieces, about 2–3 cm/1 inch square. Layer up the spicy beans over the warm tortillas, then add pieces of cooked salmon and top it up with the pickled red onions and sliced jalapeños.

Tex-Mex Veggie Tacos
with salsa & chipotle mayonnaise

This dish is a riot of colour, flavours and textures. You could fill the tacos before you serve them, but it creates such a lovely, relaxed dining experience when you lay everything out so that everyone can dive in and fill their own.

- 1 large sweet potato, peeled and cut into chunks
- 1 small butternut squash, peeled, deseeded and cut into chunks
- 1 red (bell) pepper, deseeded and diced
- 2 corn on the cob/ears of corn
- 4 tablespoons olive oil
- 2 garlic cloves, grated
- 1 tablespoon paprika
- 1 tablespoon freshly chopped rosemary
- 1 x 400-g/14-oz. can red kidney beans
- 8 crunchy taco shells
- a small bunch of freshly chopped parsley
- 2 handfuls of shredded iceberg lettuce, to serve

TOMATO SALSA

- 200 g/7 oz. cherry tomatoes
- 1 small red onion
- juice of 1 lime
- small bunch of freshly chopped coriander/cilantro
- handful of fresh mint leaves, roughly torn

CHIPOTLE MAYONNAISE

- 2 teaspoons chipotle paste
- 240 g/1 cup mayonnaise (normal or vegan)

SERVES 4

Preheat the oven to 190°C (375°F) Gas 5.

Scatter the sweet potato, butternut squash and red pepper over the base of a large sheet pan. Stand the corn cobs on a board and remove the corn using a sharp knife and a downward motion. Scatter the sweetcorn kernels over the vegetables in the pan. Drizzle everything with the olive oil, sprinkle in the grated garlic, paprika and rosemary. Transfer to the oven and roast for about 25 minutes until the sweet potato and squash are soft.

Remove the pan from the oven. Drain and rinse the kidney beans and add to the vegetables, then push everything up the pan slightly, so that you can tuck the taco shells across one end. Return the pan to the oven for about 3–4 minutes, until the tacos are crisp and the beans are heated through. Stir the parsley into the vegetables.

For the tomato salsa, coarsely chop the tomatoes and put them into a bowl. Peel and thinly slice the onion and stir it into the tomatoes. Squeeze in the lime juice and add the coriander/cilantro and torn mint leaves.

For the chipotle mayonnaise, mix the chipotle paste and mayonnaise together.

Place a little shredded lettuce into the base of each taco, pile with the vegetable mix and some salsa, then drizzle with a little chipotle mayonnaise – or lay everything out on a platter and invite everyone to fill their own.

Cauliflower & Chickpea Tacos

The combination of cauliflower and chickpeas/garbanzo beans makes a healthy taco. These are easy to make, full of protein, taste great and the presentation of them looks pretty special too!

1 red onion, chopped
2 garlic cloves, chopped
1 teaspoon paprika
½ teaspoon ground cumin
½ teaspoon sea salt
½ teaspoon dried oregano
1 tablespoon olive oil
1 small cauliflower
1 carrot
250 g/1½ cups canned chickpeas/garbanzo beans, drained

SERVE WITH
50 g/½ cup finely chopped white onion
35 g/⅔ cup finely chopped coriander/cilantro
12–16 flour or corn tortillas, warmed
Guacamole (see page 90)
6 radishes, thinly sliced

SERVES 6

Preheat the oven to 200°C (400°F) Gas 6 and grease a baking sheet with a little oil.

Place the red onion and garlic in a medium bowl with the paprika, ground cumin, salt, oregano, oil and 2 tablespoons of water and mix well.

Remove the leaves from the cauliflower and cut it into small florets.

Peel the carrot and remove the ends. Cut the carrot in half lengthways, then cut each half in two again. Slice into pieces that resemble small cubes.

Put the chickpeas, cauliflower and carrot into the mixing bowl and stir the mixture to make sure the vegetables are covered with the seasoning.

Spread out the mixture on the greased baking sheet and roast in the preheated oven for 35–40 minutes until the cauliflower is tender.

Mix the chopped onion and coriander together in a bowl. Place a generous spoonful of the cauliflower mixture on each warmed tortilla and serve with the onion-coriander mix, Guacamole and sliced radishes.

Build-Your-Own Taco Board

These are super easy and lots of fun to put together. This recipe uses minced/ground beef but turkey, lamb, pork or a plant-based substitute will also work perfectly. Or try using any of the taco fillings in this chapter – they'll all work brilliantly.

16 taco shells
200 g/7 oz. guacamole (store-bought or see recipe on page 90)
200 g/7 oz. sour cream
200 g/7 oz. tomato salsa (store-bought or see recipe on page 68)
200 g/2 cups grated/shredded cheese (mild Cheddar, feta or any hard cheese)
2 limes, quartered
50 g/2 oz. jarred jalapeños
1 red onion, finely sliced
1 Little Gem/Boston lettuce

TACOS

1 kg/2 lb. 4 oz. minced/ground beef
2 onions, diced
2 garlic cloves, crushed
1 tablespoon olive oil
4 tablespoons tomato ketchup
1 tablespoon Worcestershire sauce
3 tomatoes, diced
3 tablespoons Cajun spice mix
1 tablespoon ground cumin
1 tablespoon smoked paprika
pinch of chipotle chilli/hot pepper flakes
sea salt and freshly ground black pepper

SERVES 8

Make the taco mix first. Fry the beef, onions and garlic in a splash of oil in a large frying pan/skillet over high heat for 5 minutes until the meat is cooked, then pour away any excess fat.

Stir in the ketchup, Worcestershire sauce, tomatoes and all the spices, along with 125 ml/½ cup water and continue cooking for 5 minutes until the liquid has reduced and thickened. Season with salt and pepper, cover and remove from the heat. Add a splash of water if it is too dry, but don't let it get sloppy.

Heat the taco shells according to the package instructions, then keep warm on a plate, covered with a clean tea/dish towel.

Heat a cast-iron skillet in the oven or on the stovetop, then reheat the beef mixture and pour into the hot skillet. Place this onto your board just before you are ready to assemble.

Lay the taco shells on the board. Decant the guacamole, salsa, refried beans, sour cream and grated cheese into ramekins or small bowls and place around the board.

Separate the leaves of the lettuce and cluster them in groups, spoon the drained jalapeños onto the board and skillet. Scatter the sliced red onion in different spots to give it some colour. Finally, fill the gaps with the limes and coriander and serve.

Huevos Rancheros

This dish is hot! It is often served for brunch with a Bloody Mary as something of a hangover cure. If you prefer it slightly milder, reduce the amount of fiery green chilli/chile appropriately – it can be as spicy or mild as you like.

- ½ tablespoon olive oil
- 8 slices of back or streaky bacon, finely chopped
- 1 large onion, finely chopped
- 1 garlic clove, crushed
- 4 hot green chillies/chiles, finely chopped
- 1 mild red chilli/chile, deseeded and finely chopped
- 4 tomatoes, skinned and roughly chopped
- ¼ teaspoon sea salt
- ¼ teaspoon freshly ground black pepper
- 8 eggs
- 4 plain 20-cm/8-inch flour tortillas
- Pico de Gallo (see page 93) or your favourite salsa, to serve

SERVES 4

Heat the oil in a frying pan/skillet and gently fry the bacon until almost cooked. Drain off all but 1 teaspoon of the fat.

Add the onion and garlic to the pan and cook, allowing to lightly brown. Add the chillies, tomatoes, salt and pepper, stir well and cover. Bring to the boil, reduce the heat and simmer for about 20 minutes, stirring frequently.

Meanwhile, fry or poach the eggs to your taste and gently warm the tortillas in a frying pan, a warm oven or under the grill/broiler.

To serve, place 2 eggs per person on a warmed tortilla and liberally spoon the Pico de Gallo over the eggs. Eat immediately!

Conchinita Pibil

This is a fantastic way of making pulled pork. Once cooked, the meat can be easily shredded with a couple of forks. Ladle the cooking juices over the meat and serve with tortillas, coleslaw and barbecue sauce.

120 ml/½ cup sour orange juice (or 3 tablespoons orange juice mixed with 5 tablespoons lime juice)

2 kg/4½ lb. pork shoulder, bone in, pierced all over with a knife

a few banana leaves, hard stems removed, soaked in water for 30 minutes (optional)

YUCATECAN ACHIOTE PASTE

2 tablespoons annatto seeds

1 tablespoon black peppercorns

5–6 allspice berries

2 teaspoons cumin seeds

2 teaspoons Mexican wild oregano

2 teaspoons sea salt

1 teaspoon ground cinnamon

8 garlic cloves, crushed

½ teaspoon finely chopped Habanero chilli/chile

60 ml/¼ cup sour orange juice (or 1 tablespoon orange juice mixed with 3 tablespoons lime juice)

TO SERVE

pickled red onion (store-bought)

wheat tortillas

cooked basmati rice

your favourite hot salsa

SERVES 6

First make the achiote paste. Put the annatto, peppercorns, allspice, cumin, oregano and salt in a heavy-duty mortar and grind together with a pestle (or use a spice grinder). When you have achieved a fairly fine grind, add the cinnamon, garlic and chilli and continue grinding. Add the orange juice and pound to a smooth paste.

Mix together the achiote paste with the orange juice. Blend thoroughly with a stick blender or in a food processor. Rub the paste all over the pork. This may stain your hands a bit, but it is worth it to get the marinade working well. Cover and marinate in the fridge overnight.

Take a large and deep roasting pan. Lay the banana leaves in the pan so that they overlap each other and overhang the sides of the pan. Put the pork on the banana leaves and fold the leaves over the top to encase the pork. Lay more leaves horizontally across it and tuck them inside the end of the pan to securely encase the pork. (If you are not using banana leaves, wrap the pork in foil instead.)

Preheat the oven to 90–100°C (225°F) Gas ½.

Roast the pork for at least 6 hours. When the meat is cooked it will come away from the bone very easily.

Spoon the excess fat off the pork juices in the roasting pan. Shred the pork, ladle the cooking juices over it and serve with the pickled red onions, wheat tortillas, rice and hot salsa.

Burritos &
Quesadillas

How to Make a Burrito

'Burrito' literally means 'little donkey' and was traditionally a way to use up everything in the larder by packing it into a tortilla. The ultimate portable snack or meal, full of sustenance.

It has taken on many influences, especially from Texas and California, and here I'm showing you a recipe that is a true hybrid of my culinary education, from Mexico, to California, to Spain and, finally, to the UK, which I now call home.

There are hundreds of combinations of burrito that you can make using the recipes in this book. By combining different meat or vegetarian fillings with different salsas and salad items, you will have a new meal every time.

To get you started, try this winning combination: black beans or refried beans, Slow-cooked Beef with Ginger (see page 67), Guacamole (see page 90), Pico de Gallo (see page 93), grated cheese, shredded lettuce, sour cream and rice.

When you have chosen and prepared your fillings, you are ready to put your burrito together!

PREPARE THE TORTILLA

Place a dry frying pan/skillet over high heat. Warm a tortilla for about 20–30 seconds on each side or until softened. Transfer to a board or plate. Now layer up the ingredients, one by one, roughly across the middle of the tortilla. You're ready to assemble your first burrito!

ASSEMBLE THE BURRITO

1 Put one hand on each side of the tortilla and lift up the sides.

2 Fold the sides over the filling to nearly conceal it.

3 Holding the sides down over the filling, use your thumbs to bring the front of the tortilla up over the filling too.

4 Gently tuck this front flap under the filling, rolling the burrito gently to coax it and the filling into a cylinder shape. Roll up the burrito with the palm of your hand. Now enjoy!

Slow-cooked Beef with ginger

Also known as *birria de res*, this dish is a bit time-consuming, but is full of flavour and, once made, can be used to produce two different dishes. As described below, it is designed as a burrito filling, but by adding extra water to the sauce, you can turn it into a great stew. Be sure to add the onion, coriander/cilantro and a squeeze of lime at the end to unlock the flavour of the beef.

1 kg/2¼ lb. diced beef
2 bay leaves
1 tablespoon vegetable oil
2 tablespoons finely chopped coriander/cilantro
2 tablespoons finely chopped onions
1 tablespoon lime juice
sea salt and ground black pepper

SAUCE
1 Guajillo chilli/chile, seeded and stalks removed
2 tomatoes, chopped
1 garlic clove, peeled
¼ onion, finely chopped
1 tablespoon dried oregano
2 cm/1 inch piece of fresh ginger, peeled
1 teaspoon ground cumin
2 tablespoons paprika
1 garlic clove
½ teaspoon ground cinnamon
1 teaspoon white vinegar

SERVES 6

Put the beef, bay leaves, 1 teaspoon salt and 2 litres/ 8 cups water in a large saucepan over high heat. Bring to the boil, then turn the heat down to low and gently simmer for about 2–2½ hours until the meat falls apart easily when pulled.

Drain the cooked beef in a colander and reserve the cooking liquid. Set both aside while you make the sauce.

To make the sauce, put the chilli, tomatoes, garlic, onion and 500 ml/2 cups water in a saucepan over high heat and cover with water. Bring to the boil, then turn the heat down to medium and simmer for 5 minutes.

Remove from the heat and transfer to a food processor with all the remaining sauce ingredients and 1 teaspoon salt. Whizz for a bout 2–4 minutes until completely smooth. Season with pepper.

Heat the oil in a large frying pan/skillet. Add the sauce and sauté for 5 minutes. Add the beef and 250 ml/1 cup of the reserved cooking liquid and bring to the boil. Half-cover with a lid, turn the heat down to low and cook for 10–15 minutes or until the sauce has thickened.

Mix together the coriander, onion and lime juice and sprinkle over the meat.

Assemble the burrito according to the instructions and suggested filling ingredients on page 64.

Steak Ranchero Burrito

Almost every big city has a Mexican restaurant that boasts a 'burrito as big as your head'. This tasty steak ranchero burrito recipe is testament to that trend and is as big in size as it is in flavour.

- 4 large tortillas
- 1½ tablespoons olive oil
- 3 red (bell) peppers, sliced
- 2 onions, chopped
- 1½ tablespoons minced jalapeño peppers
- 4 garlic cloves, minced
- 1½ tablespoons dried thyme
- 1½ tablespoons dried oregano
- 4 fresh bay leaves
- ½ teaspoon dried chilli/hot red pepper flakes
- 500 ml/2 cups beef stock
- 200 g/1 cup fresh tomatoes, diced
- 900 g/2 lb. skirt steak, cooked and cut into pieces
- 500 g/4 cups long-grain rice, cooked
- 90 g/1 cup Cheddar cheese, grated/shredded, to serve
- sour cream, to serve
- few sprigs coriander/cilantro, chopped, to serve
- squeeze of lime juice

SERVES 4

Preheat an oven to 180°C (350°F) Gas 4.

Wrap the tortillas in aluminium foil and place in the preheated oven for 15 minutes.

Meanwhile, heat the oil in a large frying pan/skillet over a medium heat. When the oil has heated up, add the vegetables, garlic, herbs and spices and sauté for 5 minutes. Add the beef stock and the diced tomatoes. Cook for another 4–5 minutes, then add the steak and rice to the sauce for another 1–2 minutes.

Take the tortillas out of the oven carefully. Fill each one with the steak, rice and sauce mixture and fold to seal. Top with cheese, sour cream and a few sprigs of coriander/cilantro. Finish with a squeeze of lime juice.

Pork Burritos with spicy pineapple salsa

1 tablespoon ground cumin
1 teaspoon ground coriander
1/2 teaspoon chilli powder
1/2 tablespoon sea salt
1/2 teaspoon black pepper
zest of 1 small orange
1 kg/2 1/4 lb. well-marbled pork shoulder/butt, roughly chopped
1 tablespoon olive oil
120 ml/1/2 cup pineapple juice
350 ml/12 fl. oz. Corona or other Mexican beer
1 bay leaf
2 tablespoons pumpkin seeds/pepitas

SPICY PINEAPPLE SALSA
1/2 pineapple
1/2 red onion, finely diced
juice and grated zest of 1 lime
small bunch coriander/cilantro
1 tablespoon jalapeños from a jar, diced
1 fresh jalapeño or other green chilli, diced

TO SERVE
flour tortillas
1/2 white cabbage, shredded
hot sauce, to taste
1 recipe Guacamole (see page 90)
60 g/2 oz. mozzarella, cubed
60 g/2 oz. goats' cheese, crumbled

SERVES 4–6

The pineapple salsa is sweet and spicy and is best eaten with this pulled pork that has been braised in pineapple juice and beer for the perfect tenderness. This is all topped off with crispy shredded cabbage, creamy guacamole and cheese.

First, make the pineapple salsa. Cut the skin off the pineapple, quarter it and cut into small cubes. Combine it with the red onion, lime zest and juice. Finely chop the coriander stems and add to the bowl. Add both types of jalapeño, including the seeds if you want it hot. Stir to combine. Stir through the coriander leaves just before serving.

Mix together the spices, salt, pepper and orange zest and dust this all over the pork.

Heat the olive oil in a casserole dish over high heat. Brown the meat in 2 batches. Return all the meat to the pan and pour the pineapple juice and beer on top. Top up with enough water to just cover the meat and add the bay leaf. Bring the pork and liquid to a rolling boil, then reduce the heat to a simmer and cook, uncovered, for 2 hours.

Check the meat and continue cooking for about 2 1/2 hours until there is only 5 mm/1/4 inch of liquid left in the pot and the meat easily shreds with 2 forks.

Allow to rest for 10 minutes. Shred the meat with 2 forks and toss it with the remaining juices.

Top the pork with the pumpkin seeds before serving with flour tortillas, pineapple salsa, shredded white cabbage, hot sauce, guacamole and cheese.

Roasted Pepper, Sweetcorn & Black-eyed Bean Wraps with chipotle dressing & avocado spread

Sunny coloured roasted (bell) peppers morph into the juiciest, sweetest delights and make a fantastic filling for these moreish tortilla wraps, when partnered with sweet, crunchy corn, black-eyed beans and ripe avocado.

- 2 red (bell) peppers, deseeded and cut into strips
- 2 orange (bell) peppers, deseeded and cut into strips
- 3 tablespoons olive oil
- 2 corn on the cobs/ears of corn
- 1 x 400-g/14-oz. can black-eyed beans
- 2 ripe avocados, peeled and pitted
- juice of 1 lime
- 1 small red chilli/chile, deseeded and finely chopped
- 4 flour tortillas
- large bunch of spring onions/scallions, sliced
- small bunch of coriander/cilantro
- sea salt and freshly ground black pepper
- sour cream, to serve

DRESSING

- 2 tablespoons chipotle paste
- 2 tablespoons olive oil
- 1 tablespoon red wine vinegar
- 2 teaspoons caster/granulated sugar

SERVES 4

Preheat the oven to 190°C (375°F) Gas 5.

Scatter the (bell) peppers over a sheet pan, drizzle over the oil and roast for 15 minutes until they are starting to soften and char. Cut the kernels from the corn cobs, add them to the pan with the pepper strips and cook for a further 10 minutes. Drain and rinse the beans and add them to the pan to warm through for 4–5 minutes.

Meanwhile, mash the avocado flesh in a bowl and add the lime juice and chopped chilli. Season to taste.

For the dressing, whisk the chipotle paste, oil, vinegar and sugar together and season to taste.

Spread each of the tortillas with some of the avocado spread and pile with some of the bean mixture. Drizzle over some of the dressing, and scatter with a few chopped spring onions and some coriander leaves. Roll up and serve with sour cream.

Potato Bean Quesadillas

With its rich combination of filling ingredients – piquant potatoes and beans, sour cream and cheese – these Mexican-inspired quesadillas make a great vegetarian meal, ideal for a light lunch or supper. Serve with a fresh green side salad made from avocado, crisp lettuce and radishes, dressed with lemon juice and olive oil.

400 g/14 oz. floury potatoes, peeled and chopped
1 garlic clove, crushed
1 teaspoon chipotle chilli paste
1 x 400-g/14-oz. can black or kidney beans, drained and rinsed
4 x 20-cm/8-inch soft tortillas
4 tablespoons sour cream
100 g/1 cup grated/shredded Cheddar cheese
4 cherry tomatoes, each sliced into 3
coriander/cilantro leaves
sea salt and freshly ground black pepper

SERVES 4

Cook the potatoes in boiling, salted water until tender, then drain. Mash the potatoes with the garlic and chipotle paste, mixing well. Season with salt and freshly black ground pepper. Mix in the beans.

Take one of the tortillas and spread half of it with a layer of the potato mixture. Top with 1 tablespoon of sour cream, sprinkle over one-quarter of the grated Cheddar cheese, top with three cherry tomato slices and a sprinkling of coriander leaves. Fold the tortilla over the filling. Repeat the process with the remaining tortillas and other ingredients.

Heat a large, heavy-based frying pan/skillet until hot. Dry-fry the quesadillas over medium heat, starting with them folded-side down, turning once, until golden-brown on both sides. Serve at once.

Weekend Quesadillas

This recipe is basically loaded scrambled eggs sandwiched between two crispy wraps, what's not to like about that? It only uses one pan, and it's a great dish for the whole family, because it's an eat-with-your-hands meal that you can enjoy lounging in the kitchen on Saturday morning, or eating in the car en route to sports matches.

100 g/3½ oz. mushrooms, finely sliced
100 g/3½ oz. bacon lardons
50 g/2 oz. spinach
4 eggs
40 g/1½ oz. any cheese, hard or soft, that you like with eggs (grated/shredded if hard cheese)
4 tortilla wraps, 20-cm/8-inch diameter
olive oil, for frying
sea salt and freshly ground pepper

SERVES 2

Heat a drizzle of oil in a medium or large, non-stick frying pan/skillet over high heat. Once hot, add the mushrooms and fry for 3 minutes, until softening and starting to colour slightly. Add the lardons to the pan and continue to fry for 3–5 minutes until the bacon is golden and the mushrooms are well browned.

Next, add the spinach and stir it through the mushroom mixture until it wilts – this should only take a minute. Scoop all of the cooked items out of the pan and on to a plate, then wipe the pan clean with some paper towel (don't wash it as you're about to use it again).

Next, whisk the eggs in a bowl, season well, then add the mushroom mixture and briefly mix. The residual heat might start to cook the eggs slightly, but that's fine.

The grated cheese is used to create a barrier for the egg mix, so sprinkle the cheese in a 2.5-cm/1-inch thick ring around the edge of two of the tortillas. Place one of these tortillas in the frying pan, spoon half the egg mixture into the centre and spread it up to the ring of cheese. Gently place a second plain tortilla on top and fry for 2–3 minutes, until the egg is starting to set and the base tortilla is crispy. Using a spatula and some confidence, flip the quesadilla over and fry on the other side for 2–3 minutes. Transfer to a board and repeat with the remaining ingredients. To serve, slice up the quesadillas like a pizza and enjoy.

Chicken Quesadillas

The word 'quesadilla' comes from 'queso' (cheese) and 'tortilla', as these basic ingredients are at the core of this dish. The tortilla must be cooked until crisp but not burnt, and the cheese inside must be melted. Just like burritos and tacos, quesadillas can be the base for an infinite number of fillings so that you can experiment with combinations of fillings. Kids love the way the melted cheese glues everything together inside.

400 g/14 oz. chicken breast fillets
Chipotle Marinade (see page 43)
4 x 26-cm/10-inch flour tortillas
200 g/2 cups grated/shredded Monterey Jack or Cheddar cheese

SERVING SUGGESTION
Guacamole (see page 90) sour cream
sour cream
Pico de Gallo (see page 93)

SERVES 4

If the chicken fillets are very thick, flatten them slightly with a rolling pin. Put in a bowl, add the Chipotle Marinade and mix well. Cover, refrigerate and marinate for 2–4 hours.

When you are ready to start cooking, preheat the grill/broiler to high.

Grill/broil the chicken for 10 minutes, turning halfway through, until cooked through.

Lay the tortillas in front of you on a clean work surface. Divide the cheese and chicken between the tortillas, arranging them in a wide strip down the middle. Fold a third of the tortilla over the filling, then fold the opposite third over that.

Place a dry stovetop grill pan or frying pan/skillet over high heat. Put one quesadilla in the hot pan, allow to brown for 1 minute, then gently flip it over and toast the other side. Repeat with the remaining quesadillas.

Cut each quesadilla diagonally into 4. Serve with Guacamole, sour cream and Pico de Gallo, if you like.

Philly Cheesesteak Chimichangas

This recipe is a sneaky fusion of Mexican food and the quintessential Philly cheesesteak that is so eternally popular in America.

- a few splashes of olive oil
- 1 large white onion, thinly sliced
- 1 green (bell) pepper, thinly sliced
- 1 red (bell) pepper, thinly sliced
- 1 teaspoon dried oregano
- 500 g/18 oz. sirloin steak
- about 500 ml/2 cups vegetable oil
- ¼ of a white cabbage, finely shredded
- 8 large flour tortillas
- 16 slices of Gouda cheese (or Provolone)
- 2 eggs, whisked
- sea salt and freshly ground black pepper

SERVES 4

Heat a splash of olive oil in a frying pan/skillet set over medium heat and sauté the onion and peppers for 15–20 minutes until they are nicely caramelized. Remove from the heat, season with salt, pepper and the oregano and set to one side.

Meanwhile, prepare the meat. Cut each piece of steak in half, lay a piece in between two sheets of clingfilm/plastic wrap (or baking parchment) and use a meat hammer (or rolling pin) to whack the steaks until they are as thin as you can get them (ideally about 3 mm/⅛ inch or less). Once flattened, season the steaks liberally with salt and pepper and roughly slice into 5-cm/2-inch wide strips.

Heat a frying pan to smoking hot, add a splash of olive oil and dump a handful of the steak strips into the pan, stir-frying as you do. Stir-fry only for a couple of minutes until most of the steak is cooked but there are still some pink bits. Use a slotted spoon to remove the steak from the pan. Continue until all the steak is cooked. I usually tip all the cooked onions and peppers back into the pan at the end to mop up any leftover flavours.

In a clean frying pan, fill with enough vegetable oil to cover the base by 2.5 cm/1 inch and set over medium heat.

While the oil is getting hot, lay out a tortilla on the work surface and place some shredded white cabbage in the centre. Top with some fried steak, onions and peppers and finally a couple of slices of cheese. Fold the bottom part of the tortilla over the top of the filling, then fold both sides in and finally tightly roll it over so it seals (a bit like an envelope). Keep hold of it and dip in the egg wash, then carefully place into the hot oil, seam-side down. You must lay the egg-washed burrito seam-side down and leave it in place for 1 minute to stop it opening. Use tongs to turn it over after 1 minute and cook the other side for another minute until golden and crisp. Continue making and cooking the chimichangas until everyone has one.

Two chimichangas per person is usually ample but they also go well with a portion of chips/fries, if liked.

Vegan Baked Fajitas

Fajitas seem like the best party food to serve to a crowd. Making up your own fajita while sat around a table with your friends or family is such a sociable way to enjoy a meal. Try the meat version on page 84 if preferred, or serve together so there is something for everyone at party time!

- 2 medium sweet potatoes, peeled and chopped into 1.5-cm/½-inch pieces
- 3 teaspoons olive oil
- 2 (bell) peppers, ideally different colours, deseeded and cut into 2-cm/¾-inch long slices
- 2 red onions, sliced into thin wedges
- 1 x 28-g/1-oz. packet of fajita seasoning mix (try to avoid those with sugar as the prime ingredient)
- 1 x 400-g/14-oz. can chickpeas/garbanzo beans, drained and rinsed
- warmed corn or flour tortillas, to serve

SERVES 4

Preheat the oven to 200°C (400°F) Gas 6.

Put the sweet potatoes on a large sheet pan with sides. Drizzle over ½ teaspoon of the olive oil. Bake in the preheated oven for 15 minutes.

Meanwhile, mix the peppers, onions, remaining olive oil and the fajita seasoning together in a bowl.

Once the sweet potatoes have been baking for about 15 minutes, add the pepper and onion mix to the sheet pan and stir.

Bake for another 15 minutes then add the chickpeas for the last minute and stir well. Serve with tortillas.

Chicken Fajitas with mild guacamole

This is a very popular and sociable meal. Simply lay all of the elements out on the table and let people help themselves. It's so delicious, you'll be hard pushed to stop your guests going back for seconds, or even thirds!

800 g/1¾ lb. boneless, skinless chicken breasts, cut into strips

2 orange (bell) peppers, deseeded and sliced

2 courgettes/zucchini, sliced

2 onions, halved and sliced

1 x 28-g/1-oz. pack fajita seasoning (try and avoid the ones that have sugar as their prime ingredient)

4 tablespoons olive oil

sea salt and freshly ground black pepper

TO SERVE

8 tortilla wraps or lettuce leaves

Guacamole (see page 90)

lime wedges

SERVES 4

Preheat the oven to 220°C (425°F) Gas 7.

In a large bowl, mix together the chicken strips, orange peppers, courgettes and onions. In a separate bowl, mix the fajita seasoning and olive oil, then combine the seasoning/oil mix with the chicken mix and stir to make sure everything is coated evenly.

Spread this mix out on a large sheet pan. Bake in the preheated oven for 15 minutes or until the chicken is cooked and the vegetables are soft, stirring once.

Finally, just before you remove the chicken and vegetables from the oven, warm the tortillas or prepare the lettuce leaves. Serve the fajita chicken and vegetables with the guacamole and the wraps/lettuce leaves. Serve with lime wedges for squeezing over.

Chilaquile Burger

This burger is a take on the traditional Mexican breakfast dish, chilaquiles (see page 29). A regular burger recipe goes from average to amazing with the addition of pepperoncini, tortilla chips and spicy arrabbiata sauce.

900 g/2 lb. minced/ground beef
750 ml/3 cups Arrabbiata Sauce (see recipe below)
30 g/2 tablespoons butter
60 g/2 cups tortilla chips
4 burger buns, split and toasted
4 slices Cheddar cheese
170 g/6 oz./1 cup jarred pickled Italian chilli peppers/ pepperoncini, chopped
salt and freshly ground black pepper

ARRABBIATA SAUCE

1 tablespoon vegetable oil
1 large onion, chopped
4 garlic cloves, crushed/ minced
2 x 400-g/14-oz. cans chopped tomatoes
2 tablespoons tomato purée/ paste
75 ml/⅓ cup white wine
1 tablespoon white sugar
1 teaspoon dried chilli flakes/ hot red pepper flakes, crushed
½ teaspoon Italian seasoning (optional)
1 tablespoon each freshly chopped basil and flat-leaf parsley
sea salt and freshly ground black pepper

SERVES 4

To make the arrabbiata sauce, add the vegetable oil to a large saucepan or pot set over medium heat. When the oil is hot add the chopped onion and garlic. Sauté for 5 minutes, or until softened. Add the canned tomatoes, tomato paste/ purée, wine, sugar, chilli flakes and Italian seasoning (if using). Season well with salt and black pepper and bring to the boil. Reduce the heat to medium and simmer, uncovered, for about 15 minutes, stirring occasionally. Stir in the basil and parsley and taste and adjust the seasoning if needed.

Form the beef into four thin 225-g/8-oz. burger patties.

Set a griddle/grill pan over medium-high heat. Season the burgers on one side with salt and pepper. When hot, add the burgers to the grill, seasoned-side down. Season the other side of the burger with salt and pepper. Cook to desired doneness.

In a medium frying pan/skillet, heat the arrabbiata sauce over medium heat. Add the butter and stir until it is melted. When the butter is melted add the tortilla chips to the pan. Gently stir the pan to coat the chips while taking care not to break them. Set aside and keep warm.

Place a cooked burger on the bottom half of each burger bun, top with the cheese, the tortilla mixture (chilaquiles) and the chopped pepperoncini before adding the top of the bun. Serve immediately.

Note: Any leftover arrabbiata sauce can be frozen for use another time.

Salsas, Sauces & Sides

Classic Guacamole

If you want a classic dip with a long history, then look no further than guacamole – originally made by the Aztecs in the 16th century. In its purest form, all it contains is avocado mashed with salt, but over the centuries more and more variations have been developed.

- 3 ripe avocados, skinned, pitted and roughly chopped
- 1 vine-ripened tomato, skinned, deseeded and roughly chopped
- 3 fresh green chillies, deseeded and finely chopped
- juice of 2 small limes
- a little extra virgin olive oil
- 2 spring onions/scallions, finely chopped
- small bunch of coriander/cilantro, finely chopped
- sea salt and freshly ground black pepper

SERVES 4–6

In a large bowl, mash the avocados, tomato and chillies together with the lime juice. The consistency should be chunky yet smooth – add a little olive oil to help achieve this. Add the onions and coriander/cilantro and mix well. Season with salt and pepper to taste and serve immediately.

Salsa Roja

This is a hot salsa of charred tomato and three classic Mexican chillies.

- 2 tablespoons olive oil
- 1 onion, finely chopped
- 4–5 large plum tomatoes, halved and cored
- 2–3 garlic cloves
- 1 teaspoon dried oregano
- 1 fresh Serrano or Jalapeño chilli, deseeded and chopped
- 3 fresh De Arbol chillies, deseeded and chopped
- 5 fresh Guajillo chillies, deseeded and chopped
- small bunch of coriander/cilantro, finely chopped
- sea salt and freshly ground black pepper

SERVES 4

Heat a heavy-based frying pan/skillet over high heat. Add a little oil and fry the onion and tomatoes hard until they begin to blacken (about 7–11 minutes), but stir as required to prevent burning. Add the garlic and cook for a further 3–4 minutes.

Transfer the contents of the pan to a food processor with the oregano and chillies. Add the remaining oil as you blend until you have a smooth and even paste. Season to taste with salt and pepper, then add the coriander/cilantro and briefly blend again to mix this through.

Place into a tightly sealed jar and allow to cool. The flavours will improve over the next few days if you can wait that long! The salsa will keep for 1–2 weeks, refrigerated. Serve at room temperature.

Pico de Gallo

Pico de gallo in Mexican means 'rooster's beak', but is also referred to as salsa crudo. The onion and chilli are marinated in the lime juice instead of being stirred through the juice at the end – this helps to round the flavour of the onion and, to a lesser extent, the chillies.

1 Serrano chilli
1 Poblano chilli
3 Jalapeño chillies
1 red onion, finely chopped
2 spring onions/scallions, finely chopped
120 ml/½ cup freshly squeezed lime juice
3 tomatoes, roughly chopped
1 avocado, roughly chopped
small handful of fresh coriander/cilantro, chopped
sea salt and freshly ground black pepper

MAKES 200–250 G/1–2 CUPS

Deseed and finely chop all the chillies. Put the chopped chillies, onion, spring onions, ½ teaspoon salt and the lime juice in a small bowl and mix well. Refrigerate for 1–2 hours.

Drain off the excess liquid from the refrigerated salsa. Add the tomatoes, avocado and coriander. Mix well and season to taste.

Green Pepper, Tomato & Habanero Chilli Salsa

Real salsas are at their best just after they are made. Once you have experienced these feisty, zingy flavours, you will never go back to supermarket salsa! Eat in burritos or with a plate of nachos.

2 green sweet/bell peppers
120 g/4 oz. cucumber
4 plum tomatoes
2 shallots, finely chopped
1 garlic clove, crushed
handful of fresh flat leaf parsley, chopped
1 Habanero or Scotch Bonnet chilli, very finely chopped
grated zest and freshly squeezed juice of 1 lime
4 tablespoons olive oil
2 tablespoons red wine vinegar
sea salt and freshly ground black pepper

MAKES 200–250 G/1–2 CUPS

Peel, deseed and dice the sweet/bell peppers, cucumber and plum tomatoes.

In a large bowl, combine the shallots, peppers, cucumber, tomatoes, garlic and parsley. Add the chilli, mix thoroughly and season with salt and pepper, to taste. Put the lime zest and juice, oil and vinegar into a small bowl, whisk together to make a dressing and add to the salsa. Toss together well and serve as soon as possible.

Salsa Brava

Salsa brava translates to 'fiery salsa'. The roasted tomatoes give it great depth as well as a creamy texture. If you find that you are getting heat but no flavour, that means the tomatoes, onions and garlic have not blackened enough.

4 tomatoes
3 Habaneros or Scotch Bonnet chillies, stalks removed
½ onion, roughly chopped
4 garlic cloves, peeled
2 tablespoons vegetable oil
4 tablespoons crushed dried chillies
sea salt

MAKES A BOWLFUL

Preheat the oven to 180°C (350°F) Gas 4.

Put the tomatoes, whole chillies, onion and garlic in a roasting dish and roast in the preheated oven for about 15–20 minutes or until evenly blackened, turning occasionally with metal tongs. Remove from the oven and allow to cool for 10 minutes.

Heat the oil in a saucepan for 1 minute. Remove from the heat, add the crushed chillies and stir well.

With a molcajete or pestle and mortar, crush the roasted chillies, onion and garlic well for 3 minutes. Add the chilli oil and crush again for 3 minutes.

Add the roasted tomatoes and pound well for another 2 minutes, then mix in 175 ml/⅔ cup water and a couple of pinches of salt. Continue to pound until all the ingredients are very well blended.

Salsa Verde

4 tomatoes
3 Habaneros or Scotch Bonnet chillies, stalks removed
½ onion, roughly chopped
4 garlic cloves, peeled
2 tablespoons vegetable oil
4 tablespoons crushed dried chillies
sea salt

MAKES A BOWLFUL

Preheat the oven to 200°C (400°F) Gas 6.

Put the chillies, garlic and tomatillos on a baking sheet and roast in the preheated oven for 20 minutes or until charred. If using canned tomatillos, don't roast them.

Halve the chillies and scoop out the seeds. Using a molcajete or pestle and mortar, pound the chillies, garlic and salt into a paste. Add the tomatillos and pound until well mixed. Add the coriander and onion and stir with a spoon. Add a little water or salt, if required.

Tomato Salsas

Nothing beats a simple, refreshing and appealingly textured relish, to serve alongside cold meat platters, atop hamburgers or as part of a Mexican feast. These four variations use the same tomato base to offer vibrant, colourful, tropical-tasting, summertime salsas that add a zing of flavour to any plate.

TOMATO, APPLE & TARRAGON

- 300 g/10 oz. tomatoes
- 1 apple, peeled, cored and diced
- freshly squeezed juice of 1/2 lemon
- 3 teaspoons finely chopped fresh tarragon leaves
- sea salt and freshly ground black pepper

TOMATO & SWEETCORN

- 300 g/10 oz. tomatoes
- the kernels from 1 cob/ear of corn
- 1 tablespoon finely chopped red onion
- 2 tablespoons chopped fresh coriander/cilantro
- 1 tablespoon olive oil
- 1 teaspoon white wine vinegar
- pinch of smoked paprika/pimentón
- sea salt and freshly ground black pepper

TOMATO & MANGO

- 300 g/10 oz. tomatoes
- 1 ripe mango, peeled, stoned/pitted and diced
- 4 tablespoons chopped fresh coriander/cilantro
- grated zest and freshly squeezed juice of 1/2 lime
- 1 tablespoon olive oil
- sea salt and freshly ground black pepper

CHILLI TOMATO

- 300 g/10 oz. tomatoes
- 2 red chillies/chiles (see Note below)
- 1 garlic clove, peeled and crushed
- 2 tablespoons extra virgin olive oil
- 1 teaspoon balsamic vinegar
- 2 tablespoons chopped fresh coriander/cilantro
- sea salt and freshly ground black pepper

ALL SERVE 4

For each of the salsas, halve the tomatoes and scoop out the soft seedy pulp, creating tomato shells. Finely dice the tomato shells, discarding the hard, white, stem base.

In a bowl, toss together the diced tomato and the remaining ingredients. Season with salt and pepper, and serve.

Note: To prepare the chillies/chiles, grill/broil them until charred on all sides. Wrap in a plastic bag (so that the steam will make them easier to peel) and set aside to cool. Once cool, peel, deseed and finely chop the chillies/chiles, being careful to wash your hands thoroughly after handling. Once prepared, use the chopped chillies/chiles following the method as above.

Refried Pinto Beans with Paprika

You will be hard pressed to find a restaurant in Mexico that does not serve its own version of this classic.

175 g/1 cup dried pinto beans
½ teaspoon sea salt
1 tablespoon vegetable oil
¼ onion, finely chopped
1 garlic clove, crushed
2 teaspoons paprika

SERVES 4

Put the dried beans and 1.5 litres/6 cups water in a saucepan. Bring to the boil, then turn the heat down to low, partially cover and simmer gently for 2–2½ hours. Add a little more water if necessary. You should be able to crush the beans easily.

Heat the oil in a large saucepan over medium heat and fry the onion and garlic for a few seconds.

Add the beans, their cooking water and the paprika and cook for 10 minutes over medium-low heat, mashing continuously with a potato masher. Add a little extra boiling water if dry, and taste and add more salt if required.

Northern-style Refried Pinto Beans

This is for meat lovers – using sausages and pancetta. A rich and hearty take on the popular cowboy beans.

1 quantity cooked pinto beans from recipe left
100 g/3½ oz. good pork sausages, cut into wsmall pieces
3 frankfurters, cut into small pieces
100 g/3½ oz. pork belly or pancetta, finely chopped
¼ onion, finely chopped
2 tomatoes, finely chopped
1 small bunch of coriander/cilantro, finely chopped
1 tablespoon vegetable oil
1 teaspoon sea salt

SERVES 4

Follow the first paragraph from the recipe opposite and then continue here.

Put the oil in a saucepan over medium-high heat and fry the pork belly or pancetta for 5–7 minutes, stirring regularly, until browned. Add the sausages and fry for 5 minutes or until well done. It is important that these ingredients are cooked through.

Add the onion and frankfurters and fry for 1 minute. Add the salt and the beans, together with their cooking water, bring to the boil and cook for 2 minutes. Turn the heat down to low, add the tomatoes and coriander and simmer for 10 minutes.

When ready, the liquid should have a slightly creamy consistency. Add extra boiling water if dry, and taste and add more salt if required.

Red Cabbage Mix

This is best served soon after making it when the cabbage still has a very satisfying crunch, but it can be left to stew and soften in the fridge for several days. A very simple and tasty accompaniment to vegetarian and seafood dishes.

100 g/3½ oz. red cabbage
1 tablespoon olive oil
2 tablespoons balsamic vinegar
pinch of sea salt
pinch of freshly ground black pepper

SERVES 6–8

Cut the red cabbage in half and then finely slice each half, discarding any tough stems.

Place in a bowl and add the olive oil, balsamic vinegar, salt and black pepper and mix well.

Chipotle Slaw

Here, smoke-dried jalapeño (known as a chipotle) provides a delightful gentle heat to go with creamy mayonnaise and crunchy vegetables.

2 teaspoons chipotle paste
1 garlic clove, peeled
150 g/¾ cup mayonnaise
125 g/4½ oz. white cabbage
60 g/2½ oz. red cabbage
1 carrot

SERVES 6–8

Place the chipotle paste, garlic and mayonnaise in a blender and blend together for just under 1 minute.

Slice the white and red cabbages as finely as you can, discarding any tough stems. Place in a bowl.

Peel the carrot, chop off the ends and discard, then grate into the bowl containing the cabbage.

Mix together the carrot and cabbage, and then combine with the mayonnaise from the blender and mix well.

Mexican Red Rice

Tomatoes give a delicate sweetness to the rice here, with a touch of heat from the chilli/chile. Serve as a tasty side dish with grilled chicken or steak and a tomato salsa.

200 g/½ lb. tomatoes
1 tablespoon vegetable oil
½ onion, peeled and finely chopped
1 garlic clove, peeled and sliced
1 red chilli/chile, chopped
200 g/1 cup long-grain rice, rinsed
250 ml/1 cup chicken or vegetable stock
sea salt, to taste

SERVES 4

Begin by scalding the tomatoes. Pour boiling water over the ripe tomatoes in a heatproof bowl. Set aside for 1 minute, then drain and carefully peel off the skin using a sharp knife. Roughly chop, reserving any juices, and set aside.

Heat the oil in a heavy-bottomed saucepan set over medium heat. Add the onion and garlic and fry until softened. Add the chilli and fry for another minute, then add the chopped tomatoes with their juices. Increase the heat, stir well, and cook until the tomatoes have broken down and form a thick paste.

Mix in the rice and pour over the stock. Season with salt and bring the mixture to the boil. Cover, reduce the heat and cook for 10–15 minutes until the stock has been absorbed and the rice is cooked through.

Corn snacks are found on street stalls all across Mexico. Either of the corn dishes below can be served as a side to anything from burritos to quesadillas.

Grilled Corn on the Cob

- **4 whole corn on the cob, husks and stray strands removed, then thoroughly washed and dried**
- **2 limes, quartered**
- **sea salt**
- **1 teaspoon medium chilli powder/ground red chilli or paprika**

SERVES 4

Preheat the grill/broiler to high. Grill/broil the cobs, turning regularly, for 15–20 minutes or until charred all over. Remove from the grill/broiler with tongs and rub lime wedges over each cob.

Generously sprinkle each cob with salt and chilli powder or paprika to taste.

Oregano Sweetcorn

- **20 g/1½ tablespoons butter**
- **300 g/2 cups sweetcorn kernels**
- **1 fresh Chile de Arbol or Thai green chilli, seeded and cut into long, thin strips**
- **1 teaspoon dried oregano**
- **½ teaspoon sea salt**
- **2 lime wedges**
- **40 g/⅓ cup crumbled feta cheese**
- **2 tablespoons mayonnaise**
- **½ teaspoon paprika**

SERVES 2

Melt the butter in a saucepan over high heat, then fry the corn and chilli for 3–4 minutes until they start getting crispy. Add the oregano and salt and cook for 1 minute. Remove from the heat and allow to cool.

Divide the corn between 2 cups and squeeze a lime wedge over each. Top with the crumbled feta and the mayonnaise, then dust the paprika over the top.

Spicy Broad Bean Salad

The spicy, pickled jalapeños provide a fantastic contrast to the beautiful fresh broad/fava beans in this wonderful salad.

400 g/14 oz. fresh broad/fava beans

1/4 red onion

3 tomatoes

bunch of coriander/cilantro

25–50 g/2–4 tablespoons pickled chopped jalapeños (depending on how spicy you like it)

1 tablespoon of the vinegar from the jalapeños

freshly squeezed juice of 1 lime

2 tablespoons olive oil

1/4 teaspoon sea salt

1/4 teaspoon dried oregano

SERVES 4

Remove the broad beans from their pods but leave them in their individual skins.

Steam the beans for 3–4 minutes until just tender. Run them under cold water to cool them down, then peel off the pale skin from all of them and discard.

Prepare the remaining ingredients. Finely chop the onion, roughly chop the tomatoes and tear off the leaves of the coriander.

Put the beans, chopped onion, tomatoes, coriander and jalapeños in a large salad bowl and add the jalapeño vinegar, lime juice, olive oil, salt and oregano. Mix well and serve.

Chayote & Grapefruit Salad

Chayote (or chow chow as it is sometimes known) is a member of the gourd family. It has a mild taste but this means that it happily absorbs and takes on the flavours of the lime, paprika and salt in this salad. The goal here is to cook it just enough to soften it but still leave it with a delightful crunch.

3 tablespoons shelled pumpkin seeds
1 chayote (see Note below)
1 pink grapefruit or orange
1 small bunch of coriander/cilantro, chopped
1 tablespoon lime juice
2 tablespoons olive oil
1/4 red onion, very thinly sliced
20 g/3 cups rocket/arugula
pinch of paprika
pinch of sea salt

SERVES 2

Put the pumpkin seeds in a dry frying pan over low heat. Stir continuously for 7–10 minutes, taking care not to let them burn. Remove from the heat and set aside.

Put the whole chayote in a saucepan, and cover with water. Bring to the boil, then simmer for 10 minutes. Drain and set aside to cool slightly.

When the chayote has cooled, cut it in half, remove the stone and cut each half into thin wedges.

Peel the grapefruit, remove the bitter white pith and cut the flesh into neat segments.

Mix all the ingredients together in a large bowl.

Note: Chayote can be eaten raw or cooked, when it should be prepared as you would a summer squash.

GRACIAS
52

Bakes & Desserts

Three-milk Cake

Pastel de tres leches is made using three types of milk – sweetened condensed, evaporated and whole milk. The cake is an intriguing creation, managing to be both rich and light at the same time. The creamy syrup that is poured over contrasts beautifully with the fluffy texture. It is served at special occasions in Mexico.

3 medium eggs, separated

1 tablespoon pure vanilla extract

200 g/1 cup caster/superfine sugar

130 g/1 cup self-raising/self-rising flour

2 teaspoons baking powder

250 ml/1 cup evaporated milk

250 ml/1 cup sweetened condensed milk

250 ml/1 cup milk

TO SERVE

250 ml/1 cup double/heavy cream

strawberries

20-cm/8-inch springform cake pan, greased and dusted with flour

SERVES 6

Preheat the oven to 150°C (300°F) Gas 2.

Put the egg whites in a mixing bowl and mix gently with a balloon whisk for 1–2 minutes – do not over-whisk or allow to become frothy.

Add the egg yolks and mix for about 1 minute.

Whisking continuously, gradually add the vanilla, sugar, flour and baking powder in this order, allowing 1 minute between each addition.

Pour the mixture into the prepared cake pan and bake on the middle shelf of the preheated oven for 35 minutes. When it is ready, a skewer inserted in the middle of the cake should come out clean. Remove from the oven and allow to cool in the pan for 30 minutes.

Pour the 3 types of milk into a blender and whizz for 2 minutes.

Once the cake has cooled, tip it out of the pan and onto a serving dish. Prick holes all over the top of the cake with a fork.

Pour the milk mixture over the cake and allow it to seep in for 10 minutes. It will look like you have far too much liquid, but don't worry as the cake will quickly soak it up.

When you are ready to serve the cake, put the cream in a bowl and whip with a balloon whisk or electric whisk until soft peaks form. Using a spatula, spread the cream over the top of the cake, leaving a border around the edge. Decorate with the strawberries.

Cinnamon Fritters with ice cream

This addictive dessert uses the Mexican flavours of cinnamon, paired with cream, decadent vanilla ice cream and fresh strawberries.

4 flour tortillas
250 ml/1 cup vegetable oil
2 tablespoons (caster) sugar
1 teaspoon ground cinnamon

TO SERVE
good-quality vanilla ice cream
ground cinnamon
strawberries

SERVES 2

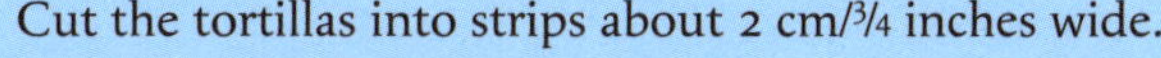

Cut the tortillas into strips about 2 cm/3/4 inches wide.

Pour the vegetable oil into a saucepan over medium heat and leave until the oil is very hot but not smoking.

Carefully drop in the tortilla strips in batches and fry for 1 minute or until they are light brown, turning the strips gently and often with tongs to prevent them from burning.

Using the tongs or a slotted spoon, remove the strips from the pan and allow to drain on kitchen paper/ paper towels. Repeat the process until all the strips have been fried.

Mix the sugar and cinnamon.

Place the tortilla strips in a large bowl and add the cinnamon-sugar. Toss together until well coated.

Scoop some ice cream into 2 bowls or cocktail glasses, stand the tortilla strips around the edge and dust cinnamon over the top. Serve with a strawberries.

Homemade Flan

Flan is a traditional Mexican dessert but it is also very similar to a dessert that is well known and loved in France and worldwide – crème caramel. As always, there are many different versions of Mexican flan, but this one has a gentle hint of vanilla.

200 g/1 cup caster/superfine sugar
410-g/14.5 oz. can of evaporated milk
397-g/14-oz. can of sweetened condensed milk
4 medium eggs
2 tablespoons pure vanilla extract

TO SERVE
raspberries

25 x 25-cm/10 x 10-inch baking dish
fluted, round cookie cutter

SERVES 6

Preheat the oven to 160°C (325°F) Gas 3.

Put the sugar in a saucepan over medium heat and cook for about 5 minutes, stirring constantly, until the mixture turns golden brown. Don't worry when the sugar starts to stick to the spoon – just keep going and it will turn out right! When you have the right colour, immediately remove from the heat. Pour the caramelized sugar into the baking dish. Swirl it around the dish until it covers the base evenly.

Put the evaporated milk, condensed milk, eggs and vanilla extract in a mixing bowl and whisk with an electric whisk on a low setting for 20–30 seconds. Pour the mixture over the caramelized sugar in the baking dish.

Boil a full kettle of water.

Put the baking dish in the middle of a larger roasting pan. Pour the boiled water into the roasting pan until it reaches halfway up the sides of the baking dish – this is a bain marie and will allow the flan to bake slowly and evenly. The resulting steam will also prevent a crust from forming on top of the flan.

Put the roasting pan on the middle shelf of the preheated oven and bake for 1 hour and 15 minutes. Remove the flan from the oven and allow it to cool for 1 hour.

Carefully run a knife around the edge of the flan to loosen it from the sides of the baking dish. Place a large plate face down over the baking dish. Carefully flip both over, then lay on a surface. Ease off the baking dish.

Using the cookie cutter, stamp out as many discs as possible from the flan. Slide a spatula underneath each disc and transfer to individual plates. Alternatively, cut the flan into 6 portions.

Pour some of the caramelized liquid from the baking dish on top of each flan and serve with raspberries.

Cinnamon, Tortilla & Ice Cream Tacos

This fun dessert combines vanilla ice cream and fresh strawberries loaded into crisp tortillas, but can be adapted to use any fruit and flavour of ice cream that you prefer.

- 160 g/1 cup chocolate chips
- 2 tablespoons butter
- 10 strawberries
- 3 tablespoons caster or granulated sugar
- 1 teaspoon ground cinnamon
- 500 ml/2 cups vegetable oil
- 6 flour tortillas

SERVE WITH

- vanilla ice cream
- chocolate syrup
- whipped cream (your choice of freshly whipped or from a can)
- fresh mint leaves, to decorate

SERVES 3–4

Half-fill a small saucepan with water and bring to a simmer. Place a heatproof bowl on the top of the saucepan so that it rests on the rim of the pan. Place the chocolate chips and butter in the bowl and melt until smooth, stirring occasionally. You may need to add 2–3 tablespoons of water if the mixture is too thick.

Discard the stems from the strawberries, roughly chop the strawberries and place in a bowl with 1 tablespoon of the sugar and mix well.

Mix the cinnamon and remaining sugar together.

Put the oil in a medium saucepan over a high heat until hot and then fry the tortillas. Do this individually, turning over 2–3 times and, when it starts to crisp up, press down in the middle with tongs to curve the tortilla on one side so that it makes a taco shape.

Remove the tortilla from the oil and place it on paper towels to absorb the excess oil.

Sprinkle the sugar and cinnamon mixture all over and then dip the edge of the crispy tortilla into the melted chocolate so that it coats the rim of the taco.

Repeat this process for all the tortillas and then transfer them to the refrigerator.

Once cooled, place the cinnamon taco shells on a plate. First fill each one with a scoop of vanilla ice cream, then cover with zigzags of chocolate syrup, add the strawberry mixture, and finally the whipped cream. Decorate with a few mint leaves.

Caramelized Apple Burrito

Softly delicious apples, spiked with cinnamon are encased in a crisp tortilla shell and dusted with cinnamon sugar. If you feel you need a break from tortillas, you can always make the filling as per the recipe and encase them in pastry.

1 tablespoon caster/ superfine sugar
2 teaspoons ground cinnamon
50 ml/3 tablespoons agave syrup
500 g/1 lb. apples, peeled, cored and cut into chunks
4 x 20-cm/8-inch flour tortilla
vegetable oil, for frying

TO SERVE

300 ml/1¼ cups double/ heavy cream
4 scoops of good-quality vanilla ice cream
mint, to garnish
cocktail sticks/toothpicks

SERVES 4

Mix the sugar and half the cinnamon and set aside.

Put the agave syrup in a small saucepan over medium heat, add the apple chunks and remaining cinnamon and cook for 7–10 minutes or until the apples have softened and caramelized.

Divide the apple mixture into 4 equal portions.

Lay a tortilla on a surface and place a portion of the apple mixture in the middle. Fold the right and left sides of the tortilla over the filling so that they overlap and the tortilla is one third of its original width. Fold the top and bottom of the tortilla to the middle so that one side covers the other and you have a shape like a burrito. Secure the tortilla with cocktail sticks/ toothpicks to ensure that the filling does not spill out.

Repeat this process with the remaining tortillas and portions of apple mixture.

Pour some vegetable oil into a deep frying pan until it comes 2 cm/¾ inch up the side of the pan. Set over medium heat and leave until the oil is very hot but not smoking.

Carefully drop in one burrito at a time and fry until golden brown, turning it gently and occasionally with tongs to prevent it from burning. Using the tongs or a slotted spoon, remove the burrito from the pan and allow to drain on paper towels. Repeat the process until all the burritos have been fried. Once the burritos are cool enough to handle, remove the sticks.

Put the cream in a bowl and whip with a balloon whisk or electric whisk until soft peaks form.

Serve each burrito with a scoop of vanilla ice cream, a generous dusting of the cinnamon and sugar mixture, a good dollop of whipped cream and a mint-leaf garnish.

Chia & Cinnamon Pancake Taquitos

Pancakes have become a popular dish in many restaurants throughout Mexico. Added chia seeds in this recipe taste great, add a crunchy texture and are crazily good for you. Served with strawberries and cream and decorated with mint leaves, this dessert looks and tastes awesome.

200 g/1⅔ cups plain/ all-purpose flour
1 tablespoon baking powder
40 g/¼ cup chia seeds
1 teaspoon ground cinnamon
2 tablespoons caster or granulated sugar
pinch of salt
2 eggs
2 teaspoons vanilla essence
250 ml/1 cup milk
1 tablespoon softened butter, plus extra for frying

SERVE WITH
fresh whipped cream
100 g/3½ oz. strawberries
2 bananas
agave nectar or maple syrup
a handful of fresh mint leaves

SERVES 4–6

Put all the dry ingredients in a mixing bowl and combine well. Put all the wet ingredients in a separate bowl and use a whisk to mix well. Add the wet ingredients to the dry ones and mix to a smooth batter.

Whip the cream to medium-firm peaks and set aside in the refrigerator. Roughly chop the strawberries, discarding the stems. Peel and slice the bananas.

Place a non-stick frying pan/skillet over low heat. Add a knob/ pat of butter and, once melted, place 4 tablespoons/¼ cup of the batter into the pan. Rotate the pan so that the mixture spreads to make a pancake about 10 cm/4 inches in diameter.

Cook for about 2 minutes, flipping the pancake over halfway through cooking, until it is brown on both sides. Repeat, using up all the batter (the mixture will make 10–14 pancakes). Stack the pancakes on a baking sheet, interleaving them with baking/ greaseproof paper and keeping them warm in a low oven at 80°C (175°F) Gas ¼ until you are ready to serve.

Lay a tortilla on a plate, place some bananas and strawberries in the centre, spoon on a dollop of whipped cream, followed by a splash of agave nectar or maple syrup, and finally some mint leaves to decorate.

AMOR ETERNO
BENGALÍ - BERESFORD
202
1327
SOMBRERO
52
S. XVI.
S. XVII.
S. XVIII.
S. XVIII.
S. XVIII.
S. XIX.
De mexicano.
Chistera.
Flexible.
De explorador.
De fieltro ancho.
Hongo.

Margaritas
& More

Classic Margarita

The original 'Tequila Daisy' is a simple yet satisfying mix of Tequila, lime and orange liqueur.

50 ml/1¾ oz. agave spirit of choice (such as blanco tequila)
20 ml/¾ oz. orange liqueur (such as Cointreau)
15 ml/½ oz. freshly squeezed lime juice
salt and lime wheel or wedge, to garnish

SERVES 1

Shake the ingredients vigorously with ice.

Some recipes call for the addition of sugar (simple) syrup; this comes from a time when the tart Key lime was the main variety available in the USA. Today, the sweeter Persian lime – a hybrid between a Key lime and a lemon – is dominant, so the extra sugar is usually unnecessary. If you do use Key limes, you might want to add 5–10 ml/ 1–2 teaspoons sugar syrup.

To serve straight-up: fine-strain the drink into a salt-rimmed, chilled cocktail glass and garnish with a wheel of lime.

To serve on-the-rocks: empty the entire contents of the shaker, including the ice, into a salt-rimmed rocks glass (this is known as a 'dirty dump'). Top up with extra ice, if desired, and garnish with a lime wedge.

Tommy's Margarita

This is perhaps the most famous variation on the Margarita. It has one small – but important – change: the orange liqueur is replaced by agave syrup, which provides the sweetness needed to balance out the tartness of the lime. It was invented after Julio Bermejo started bartending at his parents' (Elmy & Tommy's) Mexican restaurant in San Francisco in 1987.

50 ml/1¾ oz. blanco tequila (such as Hornitos Blanco)

20 ml/¾ oz. freshly squeezed lime juice

10 ml/¼ oz. agave syrup

salt or sugar and lime wheel, to garnish

SERVES 1

Shake all the ingredients vigorously with ice. Fine-strain into a salt- or sugar-rimmed cocktail glass and garnish with a wheel of lime.

BUZZ'S MARGARITA

Replace the agave spirit with honey, which provides rich, floral flavours.

MAPLE'S MARGARITA

Replace the agave syrup with maple syrup for a smooth 'like buttah' texture and a hint of nutty woodiness.

Frozen Margarita

The origins of the frozen or blended Margarita appear to go back to 1947, some ten years after the earliest recipe for the original.

60 ml/2 oz. agave spirit of choice (such as Sauza Blanco Tequila)
15 ml/½ oz. freshly squeezed lime juice
15 ml/½ oz. orange liqueur
6 roughly 2.5-cm/1-in. ice cubes
salt and lime wheel, to garnish

SERVES 1

Combine all the ingredients for 30–40 seconds in a blender. Pour into a large classic margarita glass, garnished with a salt rim and wheel of lime. Store-bought or dispenser ice works particularly well, as the hole in the middle helps it blend more easily.

Whiskeyrita

Corn whiskey gives a complementary sweetness with a touch of tortilla chips.

50 ml/1¾ oz. corn whiskey (such as Mellow Corn)
50 ml/1¾ oz. Simple Margarita Mix (see below)
6 roughly 2.5-cm/1-in. ice cubes
lime wedges and mint, to garnish

SERVES 1

Blend the ingredients for 30 seconds. Pour into a rocks glass and garnish with lime wedges and a sprig of mint.

SIMPLE MARGARITA MIX

Add 100 ml/3¼ oz. fine-strained lime juice, 100 ml/3¼ oz. Cointreau and 25 ml/¾ oz. white sugar to an air-tight bottle and shake to dissolve the sugar. Keep for 2 weeks in the fridge.

To use: Shake to remove any sediment and mix one part margarita mix to one part tequila. Serve on the rocks, or blend with ice for a frozen margarita.

Greener Pastures Margarita

The avocado gives this blended drink a creamy, smooth texture. Surprisingly easy to drink, it is impossible to have just one of these. Tajín powder is a Mexican seasoning made from a blend of chilli/chili powder, lime and sea salt flakes. If Tajín is unavailable, mix equal parts chilli/chili powder with sea salt flakes.

lime wedge and Tajín powder, for the glass rim
50 ml/1⅔ fl oz. Fortaleza Blanco Tequila
25 ml/¾ fl oz. fresh lime juice
20 ml/⅔ fl oz. agave nectar
half a ripe avocado, peeled and pitted
pinch of sea salt
3 coriander/cilantro sprigs
1 large scoop of cubed ice
purple edible flowers, to garnish

SERVES 1

Rub a lime wedge around the rim of a coupe glass, then dip the outer edge of the rim into the tajín powder. Add all the drink ingredients to a blender and blend until smooth in consistency. Pour the contents of the blender into the prepared glass. Garnish with a purple edible flower.

Strawberry Margarita

A classic Margarita with a fruity twist.

3–4 fresh strawberries, plus extra to garnish
50 ml/1¾ oz. blanco tequila (such as Don Fulano Blanco)
15 ml/½ oz. freshly squeezed lime juice
20 ml/¾ oz. Cointreau
strawberry sugar (see Note) and mint, to garnish

SERVES 1

Muddle the strawberries in the bottom of a cocktail shaker, add the other ingredients with ice, and shake vigorously. Fine-strain into a cocktail glass that is rimmed with strawberry sugar and garnish with a strawberry half and mint leaves.

Note: To make strawberry sugar, mix one part crushed dried strawberries (you can pick them out of a packet of muesli) with two parts sugar.

FROZEN STRAWBERRY MARGARITA

Add the ingredients to a blender along with six medium ice cubes and blend for 30 seconds. This even works with frozen strawberries instead of ice!

WATERMELON MARGARITA

To make a watermelon version, substitute the strawberries for 3–4 chunks of watermelon flesh.

Chelada

A Chelada (like the Michelada, below) combines the Margarita with another refreshing beverage – beer. Mexican favourites, such as Corona, Sol or Modelo, are great choices, but any lager will work. Unusually, these drinks are both served over ice.

30 ml/1 oz. blanco tequila
15 ml/½ oz. freshly squeezed lime juice
1 bottle lager beer
Tajín (spicy lime salt), for the rim
lime wedge, to garnish

SERVES 1

Add the ingredients to a tall, ice-filled glass rimmed with Tajín. Garnish with a lime wedge.

MICHELADA

Combine 2 dashes of Worcestershire sauce, 2 dashes of Tabasco sauce, a pinch of cayenne pepper and a pinch of salt before adding the ingredients for a Chelada (see above). Once again, this is served over ice, but with a rim of Sal Limón (salt with citric acid). An alternative is to use a 50:50 mix of salt and powdered sherbet.

Fresca Fiesta

This drink takes Agua Fresca (meaning fresh or cool water) as a base and adds some Margarita magic.

50 ml/1¾ oz. blanco tequila (for a heartier drink use blanco mezcal, and for a fruitier, smokier one use sotol)
20 ml/¾ oz. yuzu liqueur (such as Pierre Ferrand Dry Curaçao Yuzu)
100 ml/3¼ oz. homemade agua fresca (see opposite)
fresh mint, to garnish

SERVES 2

Add the ingredients to an ice-filled glass and stir. Garnish with a sprig of mint.

Note: The Japanese yuzu adds a lovely lemon-lime floral note, but if you can't find a yuzu liqueur, don't worry, an orange liqueur will also work.

HOMEMADE AGUA FRESCA

750 ml/25 oz. still water (cold)
2–3 hibiscus tea bags
25 ml/¾ oz. freshly squeezed lime juice
25 ml/¾ oz. granulated white sugar

Allow the hibiscus tea bags and cold water to combine in a large jug/pitcher for an hour. Remove the tea bags and add the lime juice and sugar. Stir until the sugar has dissolved and then add ice to serve.

Pineapple & Celery Water

The pineapple and celery here complement each other wonderfully to make a drink that is refreshing, healthy and very popular in Mexican markets.

1 small pineapple or 500 g/1 lb. pineapple chunks
300 g/10 oz. celery
2½ tablespoons (caster) sugar
1 tablespoon lime juice

SERVES 4

Peel, core and chop the pineapple.

Remove the leaves and some of the strands from the celery, then chop.

Put all the ingredients and 750 ml/3 cups water in a blender and whizz for 3 minutes.

Strain the liquid through a sieve/strainer and, using a large spoon, press as much of the pulp through the sieve as possible. Discard any remaining pulp.

Serve chilled over ice.

Watermelon Water

Watermelons are abundant throughout Mexico. Therefore, this drink has become common everywhere you go. It's easy to make and is very refreshing but, to serve in colder countries, wait until the summer when watermelons start to appear on greengrocers' shelves.

½ medium watermelon (about 1.2 kg/3 lb.)
2 tablespoons caster/superfine sugar
1 tablespoon lime juice

SERVES 4

Cut the watermelon into large slices and remove the seeds using a fork.

Scoop the watermelon flesh into a blender and add the sugar, lime juice and 250 ml/1 cup water. Whizz for 2 minutes

Serve chilled over ice.

Index

Credits

RECIPE CREDITS

All recipes are by **Felipe Fuentes Cruz** and **Ben Fordham**, except for the following:

MEGAN DAVIES
Weekend Quesadillas

JESSE ESTES
Greener Pastures Margarita

LIZ FRANKLIN
Loaded Black Bean & Sweetcorn Nachos
Roasted Pepper, Sweetcorn & Black-eyed Bean Wraps
Tex Mex Veggie Tacos

TORI HASHKA
Fish Tacos with Chipotle-Lime Crema
Pork Burritos with Spicy Pineapple Salsa

CAROL HILKER
Chilaquile Burger
Chorizo Breakfast Nacho Skillet
Steak Ranchero Burrito

KATHY KORDALIS
Chorizo & Three Bean Smoky Nacho Platter

JENNY LINFORD
Mexican Red Rice
Potato Bean Quesadillas
Tomato Salsas

DAN MAY
Classic Guacamole & Salsa Rojo
Conchinita Pibil
Huevos Rancheros
Jalapeno Poppers
Salsa Cruda

THEO A. MICHAELS
Build Your Own Taco Board
Philly Cheesesteak Chimichangas

HANNAH MILES
Layered Nacho Dip

DAVID T. SMITH
Chelada
Classic Margarita
Fresca Fiesta
Frozen Margarita
Michelada
Strawberry Margarita
Tommy's Margarita
Whiskyrita

JENNY TSCHIECHE
Chicken Fajitas with Guacamole
Vegan Baked Fajitas

PHOTOGRAPHY CREDITS

All photography is by **Peter Cassidy**, except for the following:

MOWIE KAY
Pages 13, 16, 57, 81.

ALEX LUCK
Pages 127, 128, 131, 132, 135, 136, 139.

STEVE PAINTER
Pages 15, 53, 73, 83, 84.

RITA PLATTS
Page 77.

TOBY SCOTT
Pages 23, 87.

ISOBEL WELD
Pages 49, 70.

CLARE WINFIELD
Page 74.